Toni Morrison

Twayne's United States Authors Series

Warren French, Editor

University of Wales, Swansea

TUSAS 559

Toni Morrison
Photograph reprinted by permission of Alfred A. Knopf, Inc.

Toni Morrison

by Wilfred D. Samuels
University of Utah

and Clenora Hudson-Weems
Delaware State College

Twayne Publishers • Boston
A Division of G. K. Hall & Co.

813.54
M835a4

Toni Morrison
Wilfred D. Samuels and Clenora Hudson-Weems

Copyright 1990 by G. K. Hall & Co.
All rights reserved.
Published by Twayne Publishers
A Division of G. K. Hall & Co.
70 Lincoln Street
Boston, Massachusetts 02111

Copyediting by India Koopman.
Book production by Janet Z. Reynolds.
Book design by Barbara Anderson.

Typeset in 11 pt. Garamond
by Huron Valley Graphics, Inc., Ann Arbor, Michigan.

Printed on permanent/durable acid-free paper
and bound in the United States of America.

First published 1990
10 9 8 7 6 5 4

Library of Congress Cataloging-in-Publication Data

Samuels, Wilfred D.
    Toni Morrison / by Wilfred D. Samuels and Clenora Hudson-Weems.
        p.   cm.—(Twayne's United States authors series ; TUSAS 559)
    Includes bibliographical references.
    ISBN 0-8057-7601-X (alk. paper)
    1. Morrison, Toni—Criticism and interpretation.   I. Hudson-Weems,
Clenora.   II. Title.   III. Series.
PS3563.08749Z85   1990
813'.54—dc20   89-20456
                                                                        CIP

To
Michael, Ray, Rudy, and William

To
Dea, Daddy, siblings, husband, and daughter, Sharifa,
whose beings motivate my creative spirit

Contents

About the Authors

Wilfred D. Samuels is associate professor of English and Ethnic Studies at the University of Utah. He received his B.A. in English and Black Studies from the University of California at Riverside and his M.A. and Ph.D. degrees in American Studies and Afro-American Studies from the University of Iowa. His scholarly work has been published in the *Negro History Bulletin, Black American Literature Forum, Callaloo, Umoja: Scholarly Journal of Black Studies,* and the *Explicator.* He is the author of *Five Afro-Caribbean Voices in American Culture, 1917–1929* and a coeditor of *"Of Our Spiritual Strivings": Recent Developments in Afro-American Literature and Criticism.* His awards include a National Endowment for the Humanities Summer Fellowship; a post-doctoral fellowship, Center for Afro-American Studies, UCLA; and a Ford Foundation Post-Doctoral Fellowship. His current work is on the eighteenth-century narrative of Olaudah Equiano (Gustavus Vassa).

Clenora Hudson-Weems has been Director of Black Studies and Associate Professor of English at Delaware State College. She received her B.A. in English from LeMoyne-Owen College in Memphis, Tennessee; M.A. in English from Atlanta University in Atlanta, Georgia; a certificate of French Studies from L'Universite de Dijon in Dijon, France; and a Ph.D. in American and African-American World Studies from the University of Iowa in Iowa City, Iowa. She is a contributor to a number of scholarly journals, including *College Language Association Journal, Western Journal for Black Studies, Journal of Black Studies,* and *Umoja: Scholarly Journal of Black Studies.* Professor Hudson is the recipient of several honors and awards, including a National Endowment for the Humanities Fellowship, a CIC Internship; Honorary Outstanding Black Delawarean; Ford Doctoral and Dissertation Fellowships and *Who's Who Among Black Americans.* Her current work is entitled *Emmett Till: The Impetus for the Modern Civil Rights Movement.*

Preface

In a 1974 interview, Toni Morrison asserted: "I want to participate in developing a canon of Black work."[1] At the time, she had published two novels, *The Bluest Eye* (1970) and *Sula* (1974). By 1977, when *Song of Solomon* appeared, Francis Taliafero reported in *Harper's Magazine* that Morrison was "ripening into one of [America's] best novelists."[2] With the publication of *Beloved* (1987), which followed the widely acclaimed *Tar Baby* (1981), her fourth novel, Morrison's critics seemed to agree with Thomas R. Edward, who wrote, "What I am sure about is that [*Beloved*] will convince any thoughtful reader, of any sex or color, that Toni Morrison is not just an important contemporary novelist but also a major figure of our national literature."[3] Indeed, Morrison has not only participated in the evolving canon of Black American literature but has done much to influence, expand, and solidify the place created by its vanguard, including Phyllis Wheatley, Frederick Douglass, Langston Hughes, Richard Wright, Zora Neale Hurston, James Bladwin, and Ralph Ellison, to name a few.

Morrison once stated that "trying to breathe life into characters, allow them space, make them people whom I care about is hard. I only have twenty-six letters of the alphabet; I don't have colors or music. I must use my craft to make the reader see the colors and hear the sounds."[4] Yet, above all, she has been lauded for her wide range of expression. She can be exuberant, patient, and delicate, and her talent is often described as formidable. Magical and musical are adjectives commonly used to describe her narrative. Morrison "lures you in, locks the doors and encloses you in a special, very particular universe."[5] Even critics who question the "moral and physical horror" of the world Morrison creates acknowledge the "wonderful richness and vitality" of her language.[6]

Morrison's spellbinding prose/poetry ("Sifting daylight dissolves the memory, turns it into dust notes floating in the light" [*Beloved*, 264]), coupled with the mysticism, black folklore, and mythology wove into her fictional worlds have led many critics to append the label "Black Magic" to her craftsmanship. Beginning with her first novel, she has captivated audiences with such conjured worlds as Medallion and the

Bottom, Darling and Not Doctor Streets, Isle des Chevaliers, and most recently 124 Bluestone Road; places where blackbirds appear unexpectedly, family remains are kept indoors unburied, warrior spirits gallop on horseback, and a ghost becomes flesh and blood. Even the names of her characters work like charms: Pecola and Cholly Breedlove, Eva and Sula Peace, Pilate and Milkman Dead, Shadrack, Guitar, Son, Jadine, Sethe, Paul D, Stamp Paid, Baby Suggs, and Beloved.

More important than Morrison's captivating style, however, is her sophisticated exploration of communal black life, specifically that in midwestern towns. Like Sherwood Anderson, she has often dramatized the idea that the conventional image of small-town America as provincial and narrow is a myth. Generally through her main characters, in particular black women, Morrison reveals the dynamic blacks who live in such towns, coming to grips with their search for selfhood in the empty, meaningless world, whether urban or agrarian, to which they belong.

Through her heroes and heroines Morrison forces readers to see the value of a life that is authentic because the individual assumes responsibility for self. "They express either an effort of the will or a freedom of the will."[7] Although she does not suggest that one can avoid life with others, she continually reminds us of the importance of "flying without ever leaving the ground" (*Song of Solomon*, 340), of accepting and performing the existential act of self-creation, and, consequently, of knowing what one must know "in order to become a complete, fully aware human being."[8] She suggests that, like the navel-less Pilate of *Song of Solomon*, the journey toward wholeness must be continual; only then will it be heroic. And, above all, this journey must emerge from one's sense of responsibility to pilot the self toward personal fulfillment, even if it means symbolically sealing one's identity in a metal box that is then appended to one's self, as Pilate does. Consequently, Morrison's protagonists are usually characters in transition, journeying through mysterious circumstances and personal histories to the innermost psyche, often to a triumphant discovery of self-hood.

Conceptually and thematically, our assessment of Morrison's work is grounded in the premise that her fictional characters are marginal (liminal) personalities who lack social, spiritual, psychological, historical, geographical, or genealogical place or center. Their betwixt- and betweenness necessarily involve them in a quest for personal and/or communal wholeness and fulfillment.

After providing a brief biography, we turn to our general concerns, which lead us chronologically beyond a formulaic summary of each text to an assessment of recurring themes, of the treatment and characterization of female and male characters, of the emphasis on community and friendship—and specifically on what we call a "community of women," and of the significance of the historical past. Furthermore, we give close attention to Morrison's propensity to invert, to turn topsy-turvy, the world she creates; to her use of folk material, traditional and nontraditional (Western, African, and African-American); and to her effort to (re)create her own lore by offering variations on more familiar tales. This necessarily includes some discussion of Morrison's use of mysticism and magic (otherworldiness) in her works.

Finding in *Beloved* a culmination and crystallization of the ideas, themes, characterizations, and style that occupy our attention throughout this study—one that suggests both the genius and competence of the novelist and the continuity that characterizes her fictional world— we offer a more detailed study of this masterpiece. Finally, we offer insights into the available critical responses to Morrison, which are cited in a select, annotated bibliography. Our work is by no means exhaustive or definitive, for Morrison's canon is still in the process of becoming.

Not only her ability to charm us into realizing the meaning of life makes Morrison so popular, but also her talent as a writer, her mastery of her craft. "A novel," she said, "ought to confront important ideas, call them historical or political, it's the same thing. But it has another requirement, and that is its art. And that should be a beautiful thing. That is the way I feel."[9] That she continues to write from this conviction—and with a tremendous degree of success—is evident in *Beloved,* which has been described as a "masterwork," in which her prose can "dissolve into hypnotic, poetic conversation."[10] Although her place in American letters is already ensured, we can only suppose that the completion of the trilogy, of which *Beloved* is the first installment, will negate any doubt about the merit of Toni Morrison's art.

We wish to thank Miss Morrison, who granted permission to quote extensively from her work and who made herself available through written correspondence, telephone interviews, and, in spite of a busy schedule, a personal interview in her home, where she was a gracious hostess. Special thanks must also be given to Dr. Ken Eble, who brought this project to our attention, and to Warren French, who agreed to let us do it. A very special thank you must go as well to friends and colleagues who read the manuscript and offered suggestions. During the course of the project our students at Delaware State College, The Benjamin Banneker Honors College, the University of Colorado at Boulder, and the University of Utah allowed us to indulge our fancies by sharing our research and ideas with them, and we acknowledge their patience here. We also wish to thank our typists Irene Johnson and Josette Price. Finally, a very special thanks must go to our families—Sharifa, Barbara, Michael, and Detavio, who made tremendous sacrifices while we worked to complete this text—and to Liz Traynor, who never gave up on us.

Chronology

1985   Premier of *Dreaming Emmett,* a play.

1987   *Beloved,* fifth novel, is published by Knopf.

1988   Black writers and critics protest nationally when *Beloved* does not receive National Book Award; it receives Pulitzer Prize for fiction.

1989   Appointed Robert F. Goheen Professor in the Humanities, Princeton University.

Chapter One

"As Big as Life": The World of Toni Morrison

"I am really happy when I read something, particularly about black people, when it is not so simple minded . . . when it is not set up in some sociological equation where all the villains do this and all the whites are heroes, because it just makes black people boring; and they are not. I have never met yet a boring black person. All you have to do is scratch the surface and you will see. And that is because of the way they look at life."[1]

This is Toni Morrison talking about her work. Her characters, she explains, are not "bigger than life," as some critics would have us believe, but "as big as life." Confessing to a fascination with the complication of black life, Morrison states that above all she is interested in probing her characters' "relationship to the earth, to the society, to work, and to each other to find complexity and subtlety."[2]

Morrison is fundamentally concerned with the significance of place, history, myth, essence, and presence. Her desire to rediscover these salient elements in black culture emerged from a concern that "the world would fall away before somebody put together a thing that comes close to the way we [blacks] really are."[3] Although this statement was made in reference to *The Black Book,* a pictorial that she edited, one finds a similar concern in Morrison's fiction. It is often illustrated most poignantly through the direct relationship between her fictional characters and their domicile. Although often simple in appearance, Morrison's homes are not simplistic.

In *The Bluest Eye,* for example, the Breedloves live in a storefront apartment that "foists itself on the eye of the passerby in a manner that is both irritating and melancholy. Visitors who drive to this tiny town wonder why it has not been torn down, while pedestrians, who are residents of the neighborhood, simply look away when they pass it" (30).[4] The quality of the external structure corresponds directly to that of the individual lives of the Breedlove family. Ironically, contrary to what their name suggests, their battered lives are nourished and nurtured by the depravity, fear, hate, and oppression that each member heaps upon the other. Ultimately, they breed destruction, and love has little or no place in their lives. As the Breedlove's history is revealed, we discover that their home and lives are by no means simplistic, but in fact complex. In turn, we discover the subtle but profound insights into the human condition in general, and black life in particular, that Morrison has carefully woven into the landscape of her fictional world.

Behind the Façade

Like that of many of her fictional characters, Morrison's personal landscape has been colorful and complex. But she shelters it. Hidden far from the hustle and bustle of New York's inner city, as well as from the highways that wind their way north, Morrison's home gives no indication of who finds sanctuary within. From the street, its squat, single-leveled appearance adds to its anonymity, causing it to go easily unnoticed by even the most observant Sunday driver or evening jogger. The absence of both an address or a mailbox with family name obscures it further. With the exception of the book-cluttered vintage Mercedes Benz that stands like a sentry in front, there is no suggestion of the world of letters behind the ivy covered gate and fence.

This hideaway atmosphere provides important insight into the life of this significant American/Afro-American writer, who was born Chloe Anthony Wofford, on 18 February 1931, in Lorain, Ohio, a small midwestern steel-mill town located twenty-five miles west of Cleveland; because of the sanctity of her privacy, she confesses to spending "about 60 percent of [her] time hiding."[5] She should not, however, be described as a recluse. From her parents, George and Rahmah Willis Wofford, southern migrants who left the deep South in search of improved social, political, educational, and economic opportunities for their family, she learned many lasting lessons, paramount among which is the importance of one's personal identity and privacy—a lesson that Morrison has passed on to her children.

Perhaps this was a lesson her mother began to grasp in Birmingham and Kentucky, where she spent her childhood as one of the seven children of sharecroppers John Solomon and Ardelia Willis, before being rushed north to Ohio at the age of three to escape the circumscription of southern life. Perhaps, however, it was a lesson her grandfather had learned, first by losing his land and then by becoming a sharecropper in Georgia. Whatever the reason, the model provided by Morrison's grandparents was indelible, for it continues to be a significant referent in her present life.

The façade of Morrison's house, like the Breedloves' name, belies its true nature. What appears to be the front of the house is in fact the rear, and what appears to be a single-level house is a split-level former boathouse with at least four levels. Permanently docked off the Hudson River, it looks toward a horizon of infinite possibilities that seems oblivious to and unbound by the city's skyline or the wired mesh of a towering bridge in the foreground. The pier off the patio appears to serve as a runway, offering passage and passport to a world of known and unknown realities: fact, fiction, fantasy; mystical and magical realms that converge in the world that Morrison creates. For the traveler who may choose, as Morrison does, to venture out in search of questions and answers to the complexity and subtlety of life, this setting beckons, ensuring the privacy and gateway to the past that for Morrison remain all-important.

Familial Background

Significant, too, are the other lessons relevant to sex, class, and race Morrison apparently learned from her parents, whose profound and positive influence is still borne by her, the second of four children. Their diverse personalities gave Chloe the wherewithal not only to live in America but to do so successfully. From her father, a shipyard welder, she gained a Garvey-like perspective on whites, one that left her with a distrust for them all. She readily admits: "My father was a racist. As a child in Georgia, he received shocking impressions of adult white people, and for the rest of his life felt he was justified in despising all whites, and that they were not justified in despising him."[6] Morrison remembers that her father once threw a white man down the stairs. Despite this sentiment, he impressed a positive self-image upon his daughter, while instilling in her the tools for combating what Carolyn Gerald calls "the zero image,"[7] a negative definition of self commonly associated with oppressed peoples and familiar to black children of Morrison's Depression generation. Although Morrison's father died before she began her third novel, she continues to hold up her accomplishments for his approval; he was a stickler for excellence.

On the other hand, her mother, whose name, Rahmah, was picked blindly from the Bible (like those of Morrison's characters in *Song of*

Solomon), maintained a more integrationist perspective—ever optimistic in her belief that the future would bring better race relations, notwithstanding her unyielding and direct manner in handling of offensive landlords and insidious social workers. Though on relief during the Great Depression, she remained self-assured enough to sing in the church choir, to belong to a Black woman's club, and to write to President Franklin D. Roosevelt when the meal received as dole was bugridden. Although her parents assumed that "black people were the humans of the globe," they had "serious doubts about the quality and existence of white humanity."[8]

Morrison's reservoir of significant others extends, as noted earlier, to her grandmother, Ardelia Willis, who used a dream book religiously in playing the numbers. She made her greatest impact during Morrison's childhood, acquainting her with the black lore that now permeates her fiction. Morrison confesses, "We were intimate with the supernatural."[9] The hair-raising ghost tales told by her parents—particularly her father who told the scariest—would become the genesis of the mysticism and magic that permeate Morrison's fiction. "We were always begging him to repeat the stories that terrified us the most,"[10] confesses Morrison. Similarly, her grandfather, Solomon Willis, left Chloe as legacy the memory of his skilled craftsmanship as a carpenter and his artistry as violinist. Unlike the land that he lost, his violin remained his possession.[11] This familial background, with an ambience of historical and social consciousness, mysticism, master craftsmanship, and a love of excellence and work, helped to fashion Toni Morrison the artist.

Community Influences

Morrison's foundation and sense of self were also strengthened by the cohesiveness of the small black Lorain community (about twenty-three blocks long) that parented and nurtured her for seventeen years, one she left only to go off to college. Morrison thinks of it as a "neighborhood," a life-giving and sustaining compound, a village in the traditional African sense, where myth—a "concept of truth or reality a whole people has arrived at over years of observation"[12]—abounds. Like the community in which Pecola of *The Bluest Eye* finds herself, it was a place that cared if someone was "put out" or "put outdoors." Morrison tells Robert Stepto: "And legal responsibilities, all responsibilities that agencies now have, were the responsibility of the neighborhood. So people were taken care of. . . . If they were sick, other people took care of them; if they were old, other people took care of them; if they were mad, other people provided a small space for them, or related to their madness or tried to find out the limits of their madness."[13] It is this background that convinces Morrison that there are no boring Black people and interests her in "scratching the surface" to discover the complexity and subtlety in their lives.

Education and Early Professional Life

Morrison's precocity, like that of her mother and aunt, who "explained" long division to their sixteen-year old white teacher and classmates, was detected very early. "When I was in the first grade nobody thought I was inferior, she related. I was the only black in the class and the only child who could read."[14] Although literature would become her favorite subject and reading her fondest pastime, she would study four years of Latin before graduating with honors from Lorain High, in 1949. Morrison next attended Howard University, with financial support garnered in part from the three jobs her father held for more than seventeen years. At Howard, she would change her name to Toni, participate in the drama club (the Howard Unity Players), and receive a Bachelor of Arts degree in English. Her fascination with books continued, especially the classics, which she would later teach, but she showed no real interest in writing fiction, which would later become a way of life. In 1955, two years later, after receiving a Master of Arts degree in the same discipline from Cornell University, she embarked on a teaching career as a member of the English faculty at Texas Southern University in Houston. A year-and-a-half later, she joined the English faculty at her undergraduate alma mater in Washington, D.C. There she met and married Harold Morrison, a Jamaican architect, who fathered her two sons, Harold Ford and Slade Kevin.[15]

Becoming a Writer

Although kept busy by full-time teaching of the English classics and Freshman composition, her role as faculty advisor for the English Club at Howard University, and the obligations of family-hood, Morrison remained somewhat unfulfilled. Driven by a desire to be more fruitful, she became involved in a small informal group of poets and fiction writers who met monthly to share one another's creations and invite criticism. Morrison, now thirty, initially shared her writings from high school, but these did not include fiction or poetry. She had not written any such thing, not even a short story, before working on what would become her first novel.

On one occasion, however, without a sample of her so-called "old junk," she jotted down a short story about a little black girl who longed for blue eyes. Inspired no doubt by the climate of revolution and evolving black consciousness of the sixties, a period characterized by an almost evangelical struggle for personal and racial identity, Morrison chose as the basic theme and subject of her first major work the obsession of blacks with an American standard of beauty that seemed both inescapable and destructive.

In 1965, Morrison left the corridors of Douglass Hall at Howard, where classes had included such students as Houston A. Baker, Jr., and Stokely Carmichael, and the writing group that included Claude Brown. Resigned from her teaching appointment and also divorced from her husband of more than seven years, she relocated at first to her home in Ohio, but then settled in Syracuse, New York, and joined the editing staff of L. W. Singer Publishing Company, a Random House subsidiary, as a textbook editor. She selected this job from an ad in the *New York Review of Books.* By 1967, she had been promoted to senior editor at the headquarters in New York City, where her specialty was Black fiction. She remained there eighteen years, editing some six to seven books each year, championing the careers of such writers as Toni Cade Bambara, Angela Davis, and Gayl Jones.

Although even at the point of going to Syracuse she had no real interest in writing as a vocation, Morrison was still haunted by a need for greater fulfillment of her own creative talents and better direction of her creative energies. In Syracuse, she decided to return to her short story about the little girl who desired blue eyes. She was soon encouraged by Alan Rancler, then an editor at Macmillan, to expand it into a full-length novel. Shortly after joining Holt, Rinehart and Winston, he solicited the finished manuscript, which several presses had turned down. Holt published *The Bluest Eye,* establishing the author's talent and her authoritative voice on the Afro-American experience: historically, sociologically, culturally, and otherwise.

Hence, as John Leonard contended in his *New York Times* book review, "I have said 'poetry.' But *The Bluest Eye* is also history, sociology, folklore, nightmare, and music."[16] Other critics, too, shared Leonard's opinion and enthusiasm; but what was of ultimate importance is that Morrison had finally found an avenue for meaningful self-expression and fulfillment. Although she confesses to writing both *The Bluest Eye* and *Sula* because they were books she was interested in reading but had not been able to find, writing for Morrison became "the most extraordinary way of thinking and feeling—it became one thing that I was doing that I had no intention of living without."[17] In sum, as she told Thomas LeClair, "Writing became a way to become coherent in the world."[18]

A Major American Author

While senior editor at Random House headquarters, Morrison taught at SUNY Purchase, Yale University, and Bard College, joining their faculties to offer courses in Afro-American literature and creative writing. By 1973, her career as an artist soared as the publication of *Sula,* her second novel, clearly marked her as a significant literary voice in America. This seminal work reflected the shift in the mood of society at large, where the emphasis had veered from the mass struggle for black consciousness to the personal struggle for self-realization and affirmation. The subject of *Sula,* individuation, was quite appropriate to the era in which it was published.

In *The Bluest Eye* Morrison undertook a cerebral investigation of the heroine, that in the end proved the history of the making of a demented personality (Morrison conceded that it is often necessary for one to "lose his mind to keep from going crazy"[19]). *Sula,* in contrast, lays bare the unyielding personality of a pariah, the title character, who refuses to succumb to the codes, values, and standards of both the dominant culture and her immediate environment. Here Morrison narrows her focus from the communal black experience to an intense study of individualism. We find in the text a powerful examination of the bond and friendship between two women, Sula and her alter ego, Nel, who must learn through painful experiences that one must measure the worth and acts of each individual with one's own value system based on authentic existence. As Sara Blackburn pointed out in her review of *Sula,* "extravagantly beautiful, Morrison's characters are locked in a world where hope for the future is a foreign commodity, yet they are enormously, achingly alive."[20]

In 1974, Morrison stated, "What we [blacks] have to do is reintroduce ourselves to ourselves. We have to know the past so that we can use it for now."[21] Although she made this statement just after the publication of *Sula,* she seems to intimate her thoughts at the time she was working on her third novel, *Song of Solomon*, which would receive both the National Book Critics Circle Award and the Friends of American Writers Award, establishing Morrison as a major American writer. Indeed, her statement foreshadows the theme of *Song of Solomon:* Truth compels one to get in touch with his or her heritage in order to comprehend and appreciate one's true self and establish a higher quality of existence—one that does not necessarily include or preclude material wealth. Morrison had obviously drawn from her personal history; the story of Solomon Willis, her grandfather, is the source of this work. When in the end Milkman Dead, the protagonist, finds his heritage, it is a much richer fortune than the heritage he had set out to discover. The spirit of *Song of Solomon*, we can conclude, is akin to that of the eighties, for the protagonist struggles to understand and come to grips with the historical truths, which ultimately leads to the recognition of cultural roots. Milkman's struggle is in reality a universal one, for it involves the process of self-discovery. As one critic noted: "There is more in the book than tour de force: Graceful sentences in which simple clauses bear whole themes, creating a beautiful balance between language and thought."[22] The organic combination of "fantasy, fable, and allegory," in this "wise and spacious novel," wrote another critic, "makes any summary of its plot sound absurd."[23]

Morrison's fourth novel, *Tar Baby*, also mirrors the eighties, in which individuals increasingly sought to tap their sixth sense to unravel the mysteries of the universe. Lost in a muddled life of cultural confusion that resulted from her Europeanization, Jadine Childs, the protagonist, wrestles with the notion of accepting her aborted black heritage when she enters into a relationship with Son, whose Rastafarian dreadlocks signify his firm rooting in Africaness. In the end, however, there is no resolution, as each goes separate ways.

Filled with allusion to African-American folklore and mythology, *Tar Baby* won accolades and recognition from all critical corners, superceding the previous works in the attention it won from the established circles of criticism and putting the author on the cover of *Newsweek* magazine. Writing in her cover story on Morrison, Jean Strouse said of Morrison's work: "*Wry wisdom:* In the new novel, *Tar Baby*, Morrison takes on a much larger world than she has before, drawing a composite picture of America in black and white. She has produced that rare commodity, a truly public novel about the condition of society, examining the relationships between blacks and whites, men and women, civilization and nature circa 1981."[24] Morrison was also featured in *Essence* and the *New York Times* and interviewed for an hour by Dick Cavett on national television. Toni Morrison had entered the mainstream of American literature, and her name had become a household word.

Beloved

With her fifth novel, *Beloved* (1987), Morrison's place has been expanded. Here, again, the focus is on history and heritage, for the source of the story is the *lived* experience of a former slave, Margaret Garner, from Kentucky. Above all, *Beloved* is a record of the slave experience of its main character, Sethe, and of Paul D, her later-in-life companion and lover, both formerly owned by the proprietor of the Sweet Home plantation. The concern is with the physical and psychological effects of slavery. Morrison reported that she "wanted to show the malevolence of the institution itself through a family that was devastated by slavery."[25] She does so by depicting her characters' trials and tribulations during slavery, their flight to freedom, and their life in freedom. In short, in thematics and structure *Beloved* is a modern slave narrative, but it is by no means a documentary, for Morrison succeeded in putting upon this story the powerful imprint of her own invention. A reviewer for the Book of the Month Club wrote: "I can't shake this book. It blew me away."[26]

Critics have been nearly unanimous in acclaiming *Beloved* as Morrison's finest work to date. *Newsweek*'s Walter Clemons echoes the perennial interest in and awe of Morrison's use of language that has been heard since the publication of *The Bluest Eye:* "At the heart of this astounding book, prose narrative dissolves into a hypnotic, poetic conversation among Sethe, Denver, and the otherworldly Beloved. Morrison casts a formidable spell."[27] Wilfred Sheed confirms that Morrison has not lost what one soon comes to identify as the central focus of her work, when he writes, "on one level *Beloved* might simply be read as a hair-raising parable of mothers and daughters everywhere; on another it could almost be a genuine folk tale of the period, discovered in some old trunk—the writing is timeless, and the characters epic; on any level at all it is also a unique piece of living social history."[28]

Chapter Two

The Damaging Look: The Search for Authentic Existence in *The Bluest Eye*

In Morrison's first novel, *The Bluest Eye* (1970), the pivotal idea is the domination of blacks by the existing American standards of beauty: blue eyes, blond hair, and white skin. It is a standard that is found, the narrator seems to say, at the very core of Western civilization. Those who approximate it are convinced they have acquired a "perfect ten," and those who lack it assume a "zero image" of themselves, or, according to Carolyn Gerald, an unfulfilled, insignificant, negative sense of self.[1] Morrison seems to concur when she says, "The concept of physical beauty as a virtue is one of the dumbest, most pernicious and destructive ideas of the western world."[2] The novel thus unfolds with the most logical responses to this overpowering criterion of beauty: acceptance, adjustment, and rejection. Through Pecola Breedlove, the focal character, Morrison presents alternatives and reactions to the measurement of worth by physical criteria.

From the outset, Morrison is interested in having the characters achieve a more authentic existence than those who submit to conventional standards, one that emerges from their personal efforts to realize their responsibility to become fulfilled individuals. Consequently, Morrison seems generally concerned with the significance of each character's relationship with others, particularly with the dominant white culture that provides the prevailing, acceptable images of self. Her approach is often Sartrean in that, like the existential philosopher, she reveals each character's awareness of self indirectly through his or her relationship with others, especially through visual perception or, to borrow from Sartre, "the Look." One might indeed argue that Pecola, Pauline, and Cholly Breedlove fall victim to their failure to transcend the imposing definition of "the Other's" look. Reduced to a state of "objectness" (thingness), each remains frozen in a world of being-for-the-other and consequently lives a life of shame, alienation, self-hatred, and inevitable destruction.

Pecola's Story

Set in a small midwestern town in Lorain, Ohio, during the Depression, *The Bluest Eye* tells the story of Pecola Breedlove, who, hating her black self, yearns for blue eyes she believes will make her white, extinguish her position as pariah, and give her the love and security that are desperately missing from her life. Blue eyes, she believes, are a panacea. "It had occurred to Pecola some time ago that if her eyes . . . were different . . . she herself would be different. . . . If she looked diffrent, beautiful, maybe [her father] would be different, and [her mother] too. Maybe they'd say, 'Why, look at pretty-eyed Pecola. We mustn't do bad things in front of those pretty eyes' " (40). Pecola's ultimate goal, however, is to have *the bluest eyes:* "Although somewhat discouraged, she was not without hope. To have something as wonderful as that happen would take a long, long time" (40).

To be sure, on the one hand we find upon close analysis that Pecola, a young girl in quest of womanhood, suffers an identity crisis when she falls victim to the standard set by an American society that ascribes what is beautiful to a certain image of white women. This standard has no place for Pecola's brown skin and eyes; for unlike Maureen Peal, her "high yellow dream child" (52) classmate, Pecola does not fit the mold. Whereas Maureen's complexion and sloe green eyes make her influential, winning her preferential treatment from and the admiration of teachers and peers and allowing her to wallow in comfort and care, dark-skinned Pecola is considered black, irrelevant, and uninfluential. She is ugly. Unlike Pecola, Maureen has governing influence as she involuntarily enchants the entire school: "Black boys didn't trip her in the halls; white boys didn't stone her, white girls didn't suck their teeth when she was assigned to be their work partners; black girls stepped aside when she wanted to use the sink in the girl's toilet . . . She never had to search for anybody to eat with in the cafeteria—they flocked to the table of her choice" (53).

In contrast, Pecola's classmates berate the color of her skin in a signifying verse that heaps insults on her: "Black e mo Black e mo Ya daddy sleeps nekked/ stch ta ta stch ta ta/ stch ta ta ta ta ta" (55). The exception is the narrator, Claudia, and her sister, Freida McTeer, whose parents offer the estranged Pecola sanctuary, allowing the three to become roommates and playmates.

The poignancy of Pecola's victimization arises not only from the racism and resulting interracial conflicts Pecola must encounter on the way to self-hood but also from the intraracial conflicts related to color, firmly rooted in white racist myths, subscribed to by black culture. As damaging as the white criterion of beauty that denies Pecola a positive sense of self are the values of light-skinned Maureen Peal, whose sense of superiority is associated with her color. According to Philip Royster, Maureen's behavior results from an adaptation of "mulatto aesthetics," a residue of "the enslavement and colonization of Black people in the United States and the West Indies."[3]

Pecola is demoralized when Maureen accuses her of seeing "her old black daddy" naked. Maureen claims her predominance by taunting: "I am cute! And you ugly! Black and ugly black e mos. I am cute" (61). In an effort to comprehend the unworthiness, powerlessness, and irrelevance Maureen assigns to Pecola, Claudia concludes: "Maureen Peal was not the Enemy and not worthy of such intense hate. The *Thing* to fear was the *Thing* that made *her* beautiful, and not us" (62).

The most damaging intraracial confrontation related to color, however, involves Pecola and an adult, Geraldine, whose life is defined by her efforts to escape the "Funk" she—and particular blacks of not so dark a hue and a specific orientation—associates with blackness. "Wherever it erupts, this Funk, they wipe it away; where it crust, they dissolve it; wherever it drips, flowers, or clings, they find it and fight it until it dies" (68). Though not as light in complexion as Maureen, "these sugar-brown Mobile girls" (68) live to escape and deny evidences of their black selves. "They straighten their hair with Dixie Peach, and part it on the side. At night they curl it in paper from brown bags; tie a print scarf around their heads, and sleep with hands folded across their stomachs" (68).

When Pecola enters Geraldine's home at the invitation of her son, Louis Junior, she is made the brunt of a cruel hoax. Rather than finding the kittens she was promised, Pecola receives facial scratches from a frightened cat that Junior throws at her. Properly described as misplaced aggression, Junior's behavior is retaliatory, for he wishes to strike out at the mother who failed to nurture him during childhood, prevents him from playing with "niggers," and heaps what little love she has to give upon a cat. Later, after sending the cat flying into the radiator, Junior accuses Pecola of killing it when Geraldine enters the room. Disgruntled by the injury done to the cat, but more by the presence of a little black girl in her home, Geraldine expels the innocent girl with words that cut deeper than the cat's claws: "Get out . . . You nasty little black bitch. Get out of my house" (75).

Although Geraldine's value system provides her with "order, precision, and constance" (70), its cost is a stilted, inhibited life, unwarranted cruelty to a young child, derogation, and intraracial tension. Geraldine's proclivity toward achieving a perfection associated with whites victimizes and scars Pecola: an erupted "Funk" that must be wiped away.

Pecola experiences the most damage from intraracial prejudice, however, at the hands of her abusive, negligent parents. We are told that even her mother, Pauline, decided at the time of Pecola's birth that she was an ugly child. To be sure, the onus of Pecola's negativity rests initially with her family's failure to provide the socialization, identity, love, and security that are essential to healthy growth and development. The emptiness of her parents' lives and their own negative self-images are particularly hurtful. Not only does their socioeconomic status as poor blacks set them on the periphery of society, but their perception of themselves as ugly isolates them further, offering evidence of self-hatred. This self-hatred is the most destructive element in their lives; the central element they lack is self-love.

Morrison's narrator is clear about how the Breedloves' appearance becomes problematic. It is not their ugliness, but their "conviction" of their ugliness that makes the difference: "It was as though some mysterious all-knowing master had given each one a cloak of ugliness to wear, and they had each accepted it without question. The master had said, 'you are ugly people.' They had looked about themselves and saw nothing to contradict the statement; saw, in fact, support for it leaning at them from every billboard, every movie, *every glance,* 'yes,' they had said, 'You are right.' And they took the ugliness in their hands, threw it as a mantle over them, and went about the world with it" (34, italics added).

Clearly, with such tunnel vision Pecola's parents can only fashion a childhood world of limited possibilities. Her struggles toward selfhood take place in infertile soil, leading, in the final analysis, to a life of sterility. Like the marigolds planted by Claudia, Pecola could not grow.

Commenting on what she had set out to explore in *The Bluest Eye,* Morrison identified the emotional violence heaped upon children by parents as a special concern. By portraying the "grotesque violence" done to children, Morrison explained, she was attempting to show "the nature and relationship between parental love and violence. Parents do violence to their children every day."[4] Although now a highly publicized topic, child abuse, including incest and rape, was once a socially unmentionable subject that remained unaddressed though secretly known. It is readily explored by Morrison, however, in her pioneering first novel.

Equally significant is the physical violence done to the black child by parents who are themselves confused about their identity, as is the case with the Breedloves. In the end, when Cholly rapes his daughter, it is a physical manifestation of the social, psychological, and personal violence that, together with his wife, he has put upon Pecola. (Mrs. Breedlove blames Pecola for the rape and puts her out.)

Significantly, Cholly rapes Pecola in the section of the novel titled "Spring"; he above all remains incapable of providing the fertile, parental soil a child needs to grow and develop a positive sense of self. He is without role models. "Having no idea of how to raise children, and having never watched any parent raise himself, he could not even comprehend what such a relationship should be" (126). Cholly's apparent confusion about parental love, as well as its attendant duties and responsibilities, is suggested in the actual rape itself, which occurs when he mistakes his lustful desire for pity with the love he has for his daughter. Pecola's stillborn child is not only a symbol of his personal violation but of the fettered life she has been made to live. Pecola, as Royster points out, is "the novel's central scapegoat,"[5] for she is not only made a scapegoat by her parents but also by the mulattos in the novel and even by the narrator, Claudia, a once caring friend who shuns Pecola in the end. For Cynthia A. Davis, "Pecola is the epitome of the victim in a world that reduces persons to objects and then makes them feel inferior as objects. In this world, light-skinned women can feel superior to dark ones, married women to whores, and so on and on."[6]

In retrospectively acknowledging Pecola's status as scapegoat, Claudia makes us aware of yet another individual who, as argued in Morrison's narrative discourse, is as responsible as the Breedloves, Maureen, and Geraldine. This is Pecola herself. Granted, she is taught neither that she is "free" to create herself nor that she is responsible, at some point, for choosing and defining a positive course of life. But Morrison is not silent on the subject. She indicates that a major part of Pecola's tragedy is her failure to recognize that she is responsible for defining a life for herself. Even though Pecola is a child, she has started her menstrual cycle, which makes her a "little-girl-gone-to-woman" (28). She is a "woman-child," with freedoms and responsibilities. Morrison develops this concept in her treatment and characterization of Cholly. At age twelve, he became a "man-child," assuming the reign of his life. In a "godlike state," he sought to achieve essence in a world rendered meaningless after his father had denied him. Morrison's narrator describes Cholly's choice with blues referents; Cholly's life parallels what Houston A. Baker, Jr., called a "black blues life,"[7] one that reflects a desire to find meaning from meaningless suffering:

Only a musician would sense, know, without even knowing that he knew, that Cholly was free. Dangerously free. Free to feel whatever he felt—fear, guilt, shame, love, grief, pity. Free to be tender or violent, to whistle or weep. Free to sleep in doorways or between the white sheets of a singing woman. Free to take a job, free to leave it. He could go to jail and not feel imprisoned, for he had already seen the furtiveness in the eyes of his jailer, free to say "No, suh," and smile. . . . He was free to live his fantasies, and free even to die, the how and the when of which held no interest for him. In those days, Cholly was truly free. Abandoned in a junk heap by his mother, rejected for a crap game by his father, there was nothing more to lose. He was alone with his own perceptions and appetites, and they alone interested him (125–26).

Pecola's failure to define and accept her own perceptions denies her inherent freedom and responsibility but does not negate their existence. Because she fails to realize this responsibility, Pecola fashions a life in what Sartre called "Bad Faith and Falsehood."[8] She remains dishonest with herself. This is the crucial point that Morrison's text reveals about Pecola: By acting in "Bad Faith," Pecola remains responsible, in the final analysis, for what happens to her.

Morrison's discourse thus strongly suggests that Pecola's alienation and sense of unworthiness emerge not solely from "the Other's" definition but also from her own inability to transcend the resulting reification. Support for this is offered by her response to each of the experiences mentioned above. In the scene with Maureen, Pecola's response is inertly passive in contrast to Claudia's and Frieda's, which showed they welcomed the "chance to show anger" (59). Although stunned at first by the meaning of Maureen's declaration, they collected their pride and shouted back "the most powerful of [their] arsenal of insults" (61).

Pecola, however, shrouded with shame, "seemed to fold into herself, like a pleated wing" (61). This further infuriates Claudia, who later confesses: "Her pain antagonized me. I wanted to open her up, crisp her edges, ram a stick down that hunched and curving spine, force her to stand erect and spit the misery out on the streets. But she held it where it could lap up into her eyes" (61). Similarly, when Geraldine ejects Pecola from her house, "Pecola backed out of the room. . . . Outside, the March wind blew into the rip in her dress. She held her head down against the cold" (76).

The most poignant illustration of Pecola's failure to act occurs in a central scene in the novel, when she enters Yacobowski's Fresh Vegetable, Meat and Sundries Store to purchase the Mary Jane candies she loves so much:

The gray head of Mr. Yacobowski looms up over the counter. He urges his eyes out of his thoughts to encounter her. Blue eyes. Blear-dropped. Slowly like Indian Summer moving imperceptibly toward fall, he looks toward her. Somewhere between retina and object, between vision and view, his eyes draw back, hesitate, and hover. At some fixed point in time and space he senses he need not waste the effort of a glance. He does not see her, because for him there is nothing to see. How can a fifty-two-year-old white immigrant storekeeper . . . *see* a little black girl? Nothing in his life suggested that the feat was possible, not to say desirable or necessary (41–42).

When the young child looks up she finds only "the total absence of human recognition—the glazed separateness" in the shop owner's eyes. Identifying Yacobowski's look with one that she sees "in the eyes of all white people," Pecola decides: "The distaste must be for her, her blackness. All things in her are flux with anticipation. But her blackness is static and dread. And it is the blackness that accounts for, that creates, the vacuum edge with distaste in white eyes" (42).

Embarrassed and engulfed by shame, Pecola purchases the candy and leaves. Outside, she equates herself with the dandelion weeds she passes. Like her, she thinks, they are ugly and unwanted. Although she allows her anger to surface for a brief moment, Pecola is overpowered by a tremendous sense of shame. She takes solace in eating the candy, but, more important, in symbolically digesting the smiling picture of the blue-eyed, blond-haired little girl that adorns its wrapper: "She eats the candy, and its sweetness is good. To eat the candy is somehow to eat the eyes, eat Mary Jane. Love Mary Jane. Be Mary Jane" (43).

The Sartrean Influence

A careful examination of the encounter between Pecola and Yacobowski reveals a central trope in the novel—the eyes, and their fundamental signification, which is found in Yacobowski's petrifying look. Like Medusa's look, which was capable of turning people to stone, Yacobowski's devastates Pecola, rendering her powerless and, to some degree, symbolically dead or nonexistent.

It is here that Morrison seems to be in concert with Sartre, specifically in his discussion of "the Look" in relation to the affirmation of the existence of "the Other." Sartre posits that the awareness of being seen is not only a way of affirming the existence of the other but of understanding the dynamics of the relationship with the other. One way that I affirm the existence of the other, Sartre argues, is through *le regard* or "the Look." In his now famous "keyhole" passages, he offers a vivid example in support of his argument. Imagine, he asks, that I find myself peeping through a keyhole at the activity taking place behind the closed door. Unbeknown to me, I, too, am being watched. Suddenly, I hear footsteps; turning, I meet the eyes of someone who has seen me. The meaning that the coming together of our eyes conveys (perhaps it labels me as a voyeur) causes me to suffer shame.[9]

In addition to affirming the existence of the other (I am, after all, seen by someone other than myself), the experience allows me to become aware of myself as perceived by others. I become aware of the fact that to the other I am "Object"; I am "Thing." Before my awareness of the existence of the other, I existed in the prereflective state of my freedom and my self-consciousness. In other words, I am "Subject" (immanence) for myself, or being-for-myself. Others exist as object, as Robert Cumming notes, in "the circuit of my selfness."[10] With the presence of the other, however, I come face to face with the reverse, for I am forced to realize that to "the Other, I must be 'Object.' " If he or she is to be other-as-subject; then I must be caught up in the circuit of his selfness as object.

It is, however, the consequence of this exchange that becomes problematic. As Hazel E. Barnes explains, it not only reveals my awareness of my object side but also serves as a vehicle through which I am judged and categorized. "The Look," Barnes contends, "identifies me with my external acts and appearances, with my self for others. It threatens, by ignoring my free subjectivity, to reduce me to the status of a thing in the world . . . It reveals my physical and psychic vulnerability, my fragility."[11] Thus, my vulnerability lies in my response to "the Look," as I do so with either shame or pride. Therein lies the crucial element: When the response is shame, it is detrimental because it is shame of the self; overpowered by "the Look," I forfeit my being-for-myself and become a being-for-the-other.

Pecola's Problems

Returning now to Morrison's text, we must first assess the Pecola that we meet before the encounter with Yacobowski. We are better able to understand who she is by noting that, from the outset, she lacks a sense of place. We learn this from Claudia, who tells us, in explaining Pecola's reason for coming to live with her family, that Mrs. McTeer had referred to Pecola as a "case." A ward of the county, Pecola had no place of residence. In fact, we learn that because of the fragmentation of the Breedlove family Pecola had been *put outdoors*. The crucial difference between being *put out* and being *put outdoors* is evident in Claudia's amplification. The former means that one has alternatives, the latter means that "there is no place to go" (18). Thus, Pecola's essential invisibility symbolizes her status as object within the community and her family; although present, she is not "seen" by them. Reified, she remains estranged and alienated.

The scene with Yacobowski, upon careful examination, bears her reification out. It is important to note that Pecola, engrossed at first with the thought of the sweetness of the candy, can be said to be in a state of pure consciousness. She is conscious only of herself. Although we already know about her self-hatred, we do not, at this moment, see her suffering from a negative self-concept. She is concerned only with the candy. At the moment she encounters Yacobowski's blue eyes, however, the entire scene changes: Pecola exits the sanctuary of her thoughts and enters the open battlefield the market becomes. Ironically, the shopkeeper feels "he does not need to waste the effort of a glance (42)." Yet it hits a bull's eye. Although a little black child stands physically in front of the vendor, his deflating glance says, socially speaking, no one is there. To him, there is "nothing [no-thing] to see." His glance achieves its purpose of identifying and negating the "object" perceived.

It is Pecola's response to Yacobowski, however, that is crucially important. She inteprets his action as distaste for her blackness, which signifies that the color of her skin is "static and dread." Just as she devoured (internalized) the physical characteristics of the little white girl pictured on the Mary Jane candy wrapper, Pecola in her shame reveals that she imbibes the store owner's look and the signification it conveys, not only for him but for all whites.

It is not surprising that once outside she equates herself with the dandelion weeds she passes. Paradoxically, she had earlier noted their herbal and medicinal qualities, a focus that emphasized their more positive properties. But the new focus is negative, for she sees in their whites and yellows (white skin, blond hair) the colors of her obsession as well as those of Yacobowski's rejection. Having encountered, so to speak, the eyes of the Gorgon, Pecola acquiesces; she never glances back or speaks out, but instead points with her finger at what she wishes, that is, to become acceptable like the little white girl on the candy wrapper. Unlike those who achieved victory by negating Medusa's look, Pecola never dons a menacing mask to deflect and return the neutralizing and petrifying effect of the look.

We have to conclude that the total absence of human recognition Pecola sees in Yacobowski's glance corresponds to her own negative self-perception. She can be only thing, object, being-for-the-other. With this as her central standpoint, Pecola seems able to respond only with shame; and, as noted above, shame means that the individual allows him- or herself to be defined by "the Other." Yet, according to Morrison's narrator options remain. Pecola can easily choose anger, for "anger stirs and wakes in her; it opens its mouth, and like the hot-mouthed puppy, laps up the dredges of her shame" (43). In one of the few places where the author seems to intrude to admonish, we are told: "Anger is better. *There is a sense of being in anger.* A reality and presence. An awareness of worth. It is a lovely surging" (43, italics added). But rather than choosing this creative act Pecola acquiesces and thus is consumed by shame: "The anger will not hold; the puppy is too easily surfeited. Its thirst too quickly quenched, it sleeps. *The shame wells up again, its muddy rivulets seeping into her eyes.* What to do before the tears come. She remembers the Mary Jane" (43, italics added). In her narcoleptic state of self-hatred, Pecola takes solace in shame, abnegating her responsibility for self to Yacobowski. This is indeed a castrating act of "Bad Faith."

The Communities of Women

Central to Morrison's development and treatment of Pecola's quest for authenticity is the inclusion of several communities of women against which Pecola's life of inauthenticity must be mirrored and measured, although their lives are also peripheral to mainstream society. They choose to be outsiders and demonstrate their choice as nonconformists. Thus, although they are metaphorically "put out," they have not, unlike Pecola, been "put outdoors." Representing diverse age groups, these women seem to provide clear alternatives that are available to Pecola.

The three prostitutes, China, Poland, and Miss Marie (Maginot Line), are middle-aged women whose forte is their spirit of noncompliance. In the discourse, what is significant is not the values or questions of morality associated with their lives as "fancy women." They are self-employed people who control their business; they are independent and self-reliant. Though no longer young, they do not appear squandered or devastated. They are social pariahs, yet they are not devoid of self-confidence.

In spite of their unconventionality, and of Claudia's suspicion that the women might not be happy, Poland, China, and Miss Marie live lives that appear more fulfilling than those of Geraldine, Mrs. McTeer, or certainly Mrs. Breedlove, a surname that could have been given to them. Though the blues is part of the impetus of their lives, it is not the only source of their creative energies. Discovering at an early age that men would seek pleasure from them, and rejecting the traditional domestic roles that they were expected to play, the three women choose, upon coming to maturity, to be compensated for their physical love; and they do so almost "with a vengeance" (48). The narrator explains: "these women hated men, all men, *without shame, apology, or discrimination*" (47). Here, again, we find anger and hate, when not aimed at the self, functioning as creative forces. They make the women unyielding to the point of insubordination and conceit. When Pecola asks Miss Marie why her many boyfriends love her, she responds: "What else they gone do? They know I am rich and good looking" (45).

The women's sense of experience and wholeness can be seen in their names, Marie's propensity to season her narrative with references to "soul food," and their home. Although they, like the Breedloves, live in a storefront, they live above the squalor. Downstairs, Pecola suffocates in a home of displaced and fragmented lives. Upstairs, she finds sanctuary amidst the aroma of Miss Marie's kitchen, the gut-level laughter of the women, and Poland's blues song, sung in a voice that is "sweet and hard, like new strawberries" (43). Paradoxically, it is the only place Pecola can find genuine love. Unlike Mrs. Breedlove, who both ignores Pecola and shows preference for her little white charge,

Miss Marie takes almost maternal interest in the exiled child. She greets her, "Hi, dumplin'. Where your socks?" (44). Marie's names for Pecola—Chittlin', Puddin', Chicken, and Honey—further signify her tenderness toward the child; "her epithets were fond ones chosen from menus and dishes that were forever uppermost in her mind" (44).

Generally referred to as "soul food," Marie's epithets must also be associated with the tender loving care required in preparing the delicacies that were once considered the refuse of the slave master's kitchen. Not surprisingly, Keith Byerman sees the women as "the primary . . . figures in the novel," whose song, tales, and laughter enable them to "transcend the private obsession of [the] other characters."[12]

Although Byerman correctly notes that their names suggest "larger than life characters,"[13] it is difficult to agree with him that their lives also reveal efforts to adapt to circumstances. Equally puzzling is Chiwenye Okonjo Oguyemi's assertion that the names evoke the helplessness of China, Poland, and France "in the face of more powerful forces" during World War II, the historical setting of *The Bluest Eye*. According to Oguyemi, "By bringing in the names of the typically defenseless in international politics, Morrison has succeeded in broadening her theme and making universal an existential problem in which the strong prey on the weak with impunity."[14] What Oguyemi has overlooked is that these places were not annihilated and their cultural values did not crumble, a fact that speaks to their personal strengths. Significantly, two of the places, China and France, were associated with their efforts to fortify themselves against invasions, the former with the Great Wall and the latter with the Maginot Line. Perhaps because of her visible strength Miss Marie is called Maginot Line, a term that accords her respect.

Gloria Wade-Gayles is correct in her assessment of the "three merry harridans" (47) when noting that they "have no desire for prosperity [sic] or rootedness of any kind."[15] She fails to see that they deviate from her general description of Morrison's women, however, who she sees as "removed from the possibility of self-knowledge, self-expression, and freedom. The measure of their lives is the extent to which, in old age, they will be able to look back with satisfaction on their younger years."[15] Marie's present life is marked by a greater sense of joy than her younger life. The women's present lives of venture and adventure suggest tremendous freedom, which they continue to jealously protect. Perhaps more important, they are able to form a unit akin to a neighborhood, in which the crucial element is caring for one's neighbors.

Perhaps the most significant cluster of women whose lives represent the potential authenticity available to Pecola, even in the face of impending circumscription, is the one that comes together at the time of Cholly's Aunt Jimmy's death. They unite to vigilantly oversee and conduct the appropriate ritual of departure for one of their members. Stalwart pillars of experience, they reassure one another and rededicate their lives to the welfare of one another. Upon hearing about Aunt Jimmy's illness, they "brought bowls of pot liquor from black-eyed peas, from mustards, from cabbage, from kale, from collards, from turnips, from beets, from green peas. Even the juice from a boiling hog jowl" (109). When Aunt Jimmy dies, they "cleaned the house, aired everything out, notified everybody, and stitched together what looked like a white wedding dress for Aunt Jimmy, a maiden lady, to wear when she met Jesus" (111).

This, Morrison explained in our interview with her, is a rite in which women take care of the business. They represent the quintessential neighborhood. "They are a collection there. An assemblage at the moment when they should arrive; and when they do, how they take over—because there are no agencies to do that—that is what they do . . . these women, like birds, get together and do what is adequate at the moment." Their composite lives symbolize the plight of the black woman. They, too, had edged, "into life from the back door" (109), only to learn that "everybody in the world was in a position to give them orders" (109). Although their response is to create lives that are socially acceptable, unlike those of the prostitutes, it is grounded in their own personal formula; they, too, decided to pilot their existential struggle and thereby "recreate it in their own image" (109).

Although not yet women, Pecola's peers, Claudia and Frieda McTeer, stand on the threshold of womanhood. They are further evidence of the strong assertion in the text that people—even children—must consider the direction of their lives. Claudia, in particular, is determined to overcome any definition of self that is externally ascribed. Unlike Pecola, who cuddles the images of blue-eyed and blond-haired girls that dominate her world, Claudia rejects them all and the model of socialization they represent. She confesses, "I destroyed white baby dolls. The truly horrifying thing was the transference of the same impulses to little white girls. The indifference with which I could have axed them was shaken only by my desire to do so" (22). By dismantling the doll, she responds with anger, turning topsy-turvy the negative socialization it represents.

In the end, she achieves some sense of fulfillment and authenticity because the dolls are not forthcoming at Christmas.

Thus, it is not surprising to discover that Claudia, the younger of the three girls, survived. Her survival has much to do with her carefully nurtured childhood, which she affectionately recalled:

But was it really like that? As painful as I remember only mildly. Or rather, it was a productive and fructifying pain. Love, thick and dark as Alaga syrup, eased up into that cracked window. . . . It coated my chest, along with the salve, and when the flannel came undone in my sleep, the clear, sharp curves of air outlined its presence on my throat. And in the night, when my coughing was dry and tough, feet padded into the room, hand repinned the flannel, readjusted the quilt, and rested a moment on my forehead. So when I think of autumn, I think of somebody with hands who does not want me to die (14).

With such love, Claudia would never have been "put outdoors" by her parents.

It is Claudia's inability to live a life of being-for-the-other that causes her to "out live" Pecola. Her function as narrator and our awareness of her survival are crucial. We realize at the end of the novel that what Claudia said about Pecola's experience—"The damage done was total" (158)—does not apply to the McTeer girls. Much in the manner that Claudia dismembered the doll "to see what it was that all the world said was lovable" (20), her retrospective assessment of Pecola's life emerges from her effort to see "of what [Pecola] was made" (20) and, consequently, to understand her life and by extension gain insights into the human condition. Upon dismantling the doll, she found that a mechanical dish, "a metal roundness" (21), inside the doll was responsible for the manufactured voice that made the doll attractive. Claudia comes to realize that Pecola lacked voice. Like the doll, she speaks with a programmed, appropriated voice in her monomaniacal quest for blue eyes, which in its artificiality makes Pecola ugly.

At the end of her assessment, Claudia recognizes Pecola's role as scapegoat.

All of us—all who knew her—felt so wholesome after we cleaned ourselves on her. We were so beautiful when we stood astride her ugliness. Her simplicity decorated us, her guilt sanctified us, her pain made us glow with health, her awkwardness made us think we had a sense of humor. Her inarticulateness

made us believe we were eloquent. Her poverty kept us generous. Even her
waking dreams we used—to silence our nightmares. . . . We honed our egos
on her, padded our characters with her frailty, and yawned in the fantasy of our
strength (159).

But Claudia also added, "And she [Pecola] let us, and thereby deserved .
our contempt" (158). Clearly, Claudia maintains that Pecola is equally
responsible for the role in which she is cast. In the end, she holds Pecola
partially responsible for her unfulfilled life.

It is significant that Claudia recognizes the full ramifications of her
lesson. She learns that there are no absolutes: human beings live in an
"unyielding" world. Thus, she also realizes that the approach to life she
endorses will not be definitive, as had been made evident from personal
experience. In fact, she softens her judgment of Pecola as a result.
Making a choice does not always offer a solution, she appears to conclude. She has discovered that, despite her hostility toward the dolls,
there is no fulfillment in "disinterested violence." Although she has
taken refuge in love, she realizes that "the conversion from pristine
sadism to fabricated hatred, to fraudulent love" (22) is merely adjustment, not improvement. Thus, as Cynthia Davis correctly noted, Claudia is not fully heroic because she, too, lives in an "unyielding world."
She is, however, willing to face the world more defiantly. Davis writes
that Claudia "does meet her responsibility to see (not just look), to
grasp the existence of herself and others without the evasions of Bad
Faith, and she acts on what she sees."[17]

The reason the marigolds she planted with her sister in 1941 failed
to grow was not solely Cholly's dastardly act; "the soil is bad for certain
kinds of flowers. Certain seeds it will not nurture, certain fruit it will
not bear" (160). This is the lesson that emerges from Claudia's
demystification of Pecola's life story, one learned after careful assessment. Thus, although it is "much, much too late for Pecola," who
never planted anything in the "unyielding earth," forcing it to react
and respond, it is not too late for Claudia, who continues to grow,
through her assessments, questioning, actions, and choices. She remains curious about the whys and hows of life, while Pecola meanders
among the garbage of the town.

Royster suggests that Claudia's realizations are pessimistic, but they
are not, and this is why she survives and grows. Neither does she fail, as
Byerman suggests, because "she refuses to live in her demystified knowledge."[18] Both critics overlook the significance of the narrative point of

view. Although Pecola is the central character, Claudia is the narrator, and it is her excursion into the "how" of life that sets the novel in motion.

At the beginning of the novel she already knows the answer to "process." She states: "There is really nothing more to say—except why. But since why is difficult to handle, one must take refuge in how" (9). She retells the story with the assistance of other, external narrators for amplification, doing so to approach the "why" of life that has avoided her. Her concluding comments suggest progress.

Morrison's experimentation with the narrative point of view, however, muddles the degree of Claudia's success. After posing the question of "how and why" at the beginning of the novel, Claudia explores answers, but not solely through her eyes. The internal and external focalizations, specifically with Pecola, serve to illuminate the lessons Claudia can learn in retrospect.[19] Pecola's story is merely a vehicle for Claudia's "Truth." As Phyllis Klotman correctly notes, "There is not only a progression in Claudia's point of view from youth to age, but also from ignorance to perception of the link between herself and other black women, particularly Pecola."[20]

The Ironic Breedloves

By including distinct communities of women, Morrison allows us to see individuals who refuse to be destroyed by the external definition of "the Other." In contrast, her treatment of male-female relationship themes, specifically within the Breedloves, shows the ultimate consequence of the failure to respond aggressively to circumvent a life of inauthentic existence. Using the personal histories of Pauline and Cholly Breedlove, Morrison created fictional lives that metaphorically suggest absolute absence.

Ironically named, as already noted, the Breedloves do not give life to love: familial, romantic, or personal. In fact, they destroy any semblance of it or pervert it, as in the case of Cholly's rape of Pecola. Because of their self-imposed "cloak of ugliness" Pauline and Cholly, like Pecola, were ripe victims of "every billboard, every movie, *every glance*" that offered external definition (34). They, too, are victimized by "the Look."

Prior to migrating to Lorain, the Breedloves achieve some sense of domestic tranquility. Alabama's agrarian life provides fertile ground for the rainbow of "little bits of color" (103) Pauline carried, from child-

hood, within. Cholly at first was able to resurrect the rainbow in the
adult Pauline, who derived a tremendous sense of power from their
sexual activity. She said, "I feel a power. I be strong. I be pretty, I be
young" (103). In the South, Cholly still carried "his own music" (91)
within.

Up North, however, both experience discontinuity and alienation.
Whereas Pauline found no community in which to ground herself, not
even among blacks, Cholly sought escape from industrial life in alcohol
and a community of comrades who shared a similar plight. With their
urbanization through migration, Pauline, as Barbara Christian notes,
experiences "the loss of center."[21] The marriage becomes "shredded
with quarrels" (94), as reciprocity is not possible; neither one can
experience pleasure in the other as they once did. When her dependence
on Cholly drives him further away, Pauline solicits external approval
from the "favorable glances" (94) of others, in the same way that Pecola
would.

When loneliness and boredom drive Pauline to frequent the movies,
she allows herself to subscribe to the standard of beauty which, promul-
gated by the white actress Jean Harlow, eventually leads her to "collect
self-contempt by the heap" (97). Like Yacobowski's searing look that
petrifies Pecola, Harlow's penetrating glance from the silver screen
confronts the unpolished, unsophisticated, and partially disabled Pauline, reminding her of her unfinished self. The self-hatred she already
felt as the result of her "crooked archless foot" was compounded by a
lost front tooth, and "Everything went then" (98). While Shirley Temple is a powerful social symbol for the innocent Pecola, Harlow, a
powerful signification of the society's values, affected Pauline with
Medusian stares through the very mechanical eyes (the lens) of the
movie camera. Unable to meet the required standards, Pauline confesses, "I just did not care no more after that" (98).

Pauline escapes in the clinically clean kitchen that she maintains for
the Fishers, a white family that employs her as a domestic. Here she
preoccupies herself with work, lavishing upon her employer's blue-
eyed, blond-haired daughter the love she is unable to give Pecola. The
level of inauthenticity that she reaches from her deferred life manifests
itself in the contempt she shows Pecola, who accidentally spills a berry
cobbler on the Fisher's clean, white kitchen floor. Rather than attending to Pecola's injuries, Pauline scolds her, showing more concern for
the little "yellow girl" and the clean floor than for the comfort of her
own daughter: "The little girl in pink started to cry. Mrs. Breedlove

turned to her. 'Hush, baby, hush. Come here. Oh Lord, look at your dress. Don't cry no more. Polly will change it.' She went to the sink and turned tap water on a fresh towel. Over her shoulder she spit out words to us like rotten pieces of apple. 'Pick up that wash and get on out here, so I can get this mess cleaned up' " (87).

The damage is profound and destructive. Klotman correctly notes that Pauline's action emerges from her affected vision. "Through her mother's blurred vision of the pink, white, and golden world of the Fishers, Pecola learns that she is ugly, unacceptable, and especially unloved."[22]

Pauline behaves, as both Trudier Harris and Gloria Wade-Gayles maintain, like the traditional "black mammy," popularized in plantation literature, whose love for the slave master and his family transcends any feelings she might have for her own family. Although Harris claims that Pauline is subservient and apolitical because "she remains thankful for the job she has,"[23] Wade-Gayles argues that Pauline's behavior appears more creative than destructive because her role in the Fisher household gives her desired peace and economic power. It allows her to operate from a position of strength, compensating for the sense of power she lost with the deterioration of her sexual life with her husband. According to Wade-Gayles, "In her mind, then, she is not yielding to powerlessness; she is acquiring power."[24]

Cholly, too, is bruised in a visual confrontation that involves the negating glance of "the Other." In the midst of his first sexual rite of passage, he is discovered by two white hunters who insist that he complete the act with them as audience. He is told: "Get on wid it, nigger. . . . I said, get on wid it. An' make it good, nigger, make it good" (117). The narrator explains further: "*There was no place for Cholly's eyes to go.* They slid furtively searching for shelter, while his body remained paralyzed. . . . With a violence born of total helplessness, he pulled her dress up, lowered his trousers and underwear (117, italic added).

Humiliated and scarred by the experience, Cholly internalizes his oppression, developing a distaste for his black self and hatred for the black woman before whom he has been emasculated. Thus, he responds in what Calvin Hernton sees as a classic response in some black male-female relationships: "Black men who are themselves victims of oppression [victimize] Black women with what looks like the same oppression."[25]

Cholly is able at first to forge ahead, surviving the experience and

even the brutal rejection of a father he had painfully sought, and
following the beat of the music he carries within, much like Pauline
carries her rainbow of colors. But the move north is as fragmenting for
him as it is for her. As an adult, Cholly takes refuge in alcohol to soothe
his rage and frustration. His life of inauthenticity manifests itself in
sadistic love making and the violence and brutality of his domestic
relationship. The ultimate evidence of his confused state, however, is
his vicious and tragic raping of his daughter during a confusing moment of tenderness and hatred, heightened by his drunken stupor and a
sense of impotence and guilt.

As Jacqueline de Weever points out, the Breedloves are a family that
"lives together without the structure of a strong relationship or punctua-
tion of loving gestures or deed."[26] This is most evident when they are
juxtaposed with the McTeers, who, although not much better off eco-
nomically, manage to develop a closer family unit. Succumbing to a life
for "the Other," the Breedloves destroy themselves. Their storefront
home is a veritable battlefield in which they breed daily contempt for
one another, as they abuse one another, physically and mentally.

Cholly and Mrs. Breedlove fought each other with a darkly brutal formalism
that was paralleled only by their lovemaking. Tacitly they agreed not to kill
each other. He fought her the way a coward fights a man—with feet, the
palms of his hands, and teeth. She, in turn, fought back in a purely feminine
way—with frying pans and pokers, and occasionally a flat-iron would sail
toward his head. They did not talk, groan, or curse during these beatings.
There was only the muted sound of falling things, and flesh on unsurprised
flesh (37–38).

Their beatings, rituals of the unfulfilled self, are mutual. (Pauline
confesses that she had "tried to kill him" [98] and that she had "gone
upside his head" [95].) They are less the outgrowth of "generic functions of sexism"[27] than of displaced aggression that results from their
inauthentic lives. It is not surprising that Pauline does not leave Cholly
and that she turns to religion as an avenue of retribution. The tragedy
of their relationship is suggested by the fact that she seems to understand his plight, and even defends him to a white employer who
encourages her to leave Cholly. Above all, she holds Pecola, not Cholly,
responsible for the rape, and she puts her daughter out. She also confesses, "But it wasn't all bad. Sometimes things wasn't all bad" (102).
Although we can neither approve of nor justify Cholly's and

Soaphead Church's actions, in the end we can understand how Pecola is easily victimized and raped by them, physically and psychologically. Nor are we surprised by her escape into insanity. All along, her life lacked the essence necessary "to stand erect and spit the misery out on the street" (61). Instead, as Claudia notes, Pecola "held it in where it could lap into her eyes" (61). Pecola's insanity becomes her ultimate act of "Bad Faith," for with it she finally succeeds in escaping, "folding into herself" and making herself disappear, as she had once tried to do by covering herself with a quilt while listening to her parents battle. " 'Please God . . . Please make me disappear.' She squeezed her eyes shut. Little parts of her body faded away. Now slowly, now with a rush. Slowly again. Her fingers went, one by one; then her arms disappeared all the way to the elbow. Her feet now . . . The legs all at once. It was hardest above the thighs . . . Her stomach would not go. But finally it, too, went away. Then her chest, her neck. The face was hard, too . . . Only her tight, tight eyes were left. They were always left" (39). Pecola was a "broken-winged bird / that cannot fly." "Elbows bent, hands on shoulders, she flailed her arms like a bird in an eternal grotesquely futile effort to fly. Beating the air, a winged but grounded bird" (158).

The Value of Self-Creation

In the final analysis, Morrison suggests in *The Bluest Eye* the importance of the existentially minded individual who in his or her thrust of humanity seeks first to create himself or herself. In this manner one circumvents, if not totally avoids, the fall experienced by Pecola, a "grounded bird." On the one hand, in Pecola's insanity, Cholly's tendency toward promiscuity (incest), and Pauline's escape into the world of domestic service, we find the devastating results of inauthentic existence. On the other hand, in Claudia, the prostitutes, and the community of women at Aunt Jimmy's funeral, the opposite emerges, for their lives are as fulfilling and genuine as Maggie's laughter.

In the end, Morrison is not suggesting that the victim is to blame for all that happens, in every instance. She is, however, exploring a larger question of being through the characters of this novel. In spite of the existence of "the Other," each narrator seems to say, what is important is each individual's willingness to take responsibility for his or her own life. Yet, as Davis correctly notes, Morrison's "condemnation is tempered by the recognition of the unnatural position of blacks in a racist society."[28] Morrison does not suggest that external forces, such as racism and sexism, are unimportant. We see this in her treatment of Yacobowski, the hunters, Pauline's white employers, Soaphead, and Cholly. Neither the indictment of white society for its oppression of blacks nor the indictment of blacks for their treatment of women is her sole interest or focus. As W. Lawrence Hogue notes, Morrison is concerned with "the ontological structures and mythological thought systems that blacks develop to define and reinforce their definitions of self and existence."[29] Even if it fails to grow, everyone must plant his or her own garden of marigolds. If someone else does, the seeds are bound to shrivel and die like Pecola.

Chapter Three

Experimental Lives:
Meaning and Self in *Sula*

It is in Morrison's second novel, *Sula* (1973), and specifically in her treatment and characterization of its two central characters, Sula and Shadrack, that the archetypal, authentic heroic personalities of her canon are first explored. Unlike the static lives of the Breedloves in *The Bluest Eye*, the lives of these characters are rich and experimental, for neither conforms to the prevailing social standards and values. Both fit Morrison's description of what she calls "salt tasters" who "express either an effort of the will or a freedom of the will," which, as Claudia Tate noted, makes them "free people, the dangerously free people."[1]

Unlike Pecola, who is driven by a desire for acceptance, Shadrack and Sula are risk takers who reflect "an abrogation of society with its constricting values," according to Naana Banyiwa-Horne. Sula, the critic writes, "protects herself against the mean world with a meanness which bristles against the hostility of the world. Independent, adventurous, inquisitive, strong-willed and self-centered, Sula offers a welcome, if uncanny foil to Pecola's unquestioned acceptance and futile pursuit of those values which lead to her destruction."[2]

On the surface, *Sula* is about the experiences of the citizens of the Bottom, a Black community in Medallion, a fictional midwestern town. Its central focus, however, is on Shadrack and Sula, the preoccupation of the Medallionites, who wonder "what Shadrack was all about [and] what that little girl Sula who grew into woman in their town was all about" (6).[3]

Residing with her mother, Hannah, in the house of her grandmother, Eva Peace, Sula initially draws her world view from both women. However, her inability to find meaning in the prescribed domestic roles of the women of the Bottom, coupled with her desire to be "distinctly different" (118), leaves Sula spiritually and physically alienated. "She had no center, no speck around which to grow" (103). Similarly, Shadrack is socially ostracized in the Bottom. Fragmented by his war experience, his life is a continual struggle for consistency and wholeness in the midst of isolation. In spite of this, however, both Shadrack and Sula shatter Pearl K. Bell's assertion that "the pursuit of authentic self is the last thing one expects in a novel by Toni Morrison."[4]

This central concern is muddled by the ironies, ambiguities, and inconsistencies that are endemic to the text. *Sula*'s complexity is visible, for example, in the name of the setting, for although Medallion's Blacks live in the Bottom, their community is actually located at the top of a hill, as a result, the narrator tells us, of a "nigger joke"; of "the kind white folks tell when the mill closes down and they're looking for a little comfort somewhere" (4). Located "high up in the hill," the Bottom had been given to a former slave in place of the promised fertile valley land he was to have received for performing "some very difficult chores," the dishonest white farmer falsely explained that the hilly land was at the bottom of heaven, "best land there is" (5).

There is irony as well in the structure. For example, chapter Two bears the title "1919," yet much of the action takes place before the end of World War I; very little takes place in this particular year. The most significant irony, however, evolves around Sula's and Shadrack's characterizations; although both are considered evil and psychologically unbalanced, they are, in fact, closer to being actualized individuals than anyone else in the novel.

Sula's Status in the Bottom

Sula is a pariah whose values are often the polar opposites of those adopted by her provincial society. Unlike Pecola, Sula lives out her own fantasies, creates her own realities, and sets her own personal objectives. She is motivated by a firm sense of her "Me-ness." Morrison uses Sula to question "the tendency to blindly accept existence as a given, rather than something which can be challenged,"[5] wrote Odette A. Martin. To best explore Sula's quest for authentic existence, Morrison develops her character much as she developed Pecola's: through her relation with others (Sartre's "the Other"). It is particularly through the community; the Peace women (Sula's mother and grandmother); and through Nel Wright, her best friend, that we note Sula's vigilance against the destruction of the self—that we find her fortressing her "Me-ness."

Morrison describes her intention for the Bottom community in an interview with Robert Stepto: "When I wrote *Sula,* I was interested in making the town, the community, the neighborhood, as strong a character as I could . . . because the most extraordinary thing about any group, and particularly our group, is the fantastic variety of people and things and behavior and so on."[6] Morrison's pronouncements here substantiate her premise that there are no boring black people; for above all she seems interested not only in exploring the significance of place but "the fantastic variety of [black] people," because they are never dull. Contrary to Addison Gayle's criticism of what for him is the stereotypical image of the blacks of the Bottom as "primitives,"[7] Morrison is reclaiming and, by extension, recreating a lost community. The novel begins, "In that place, where they tore the nightstand and blackberry patches from their roots to make room for the Medallion City Golf Course, there was once a neighborhood" (3).

Although "terminated and dramatically obliterated," as Susan Willis notes, the Bottom "refers to the past, the rural South, the reservoir of culture that has been uprooted—like the blackberry bushes—to make way for modernization."[8] It necessarily refers as well to the mythology, one honed in an environment of caring, that is also lost. The Bottom is different from Medallion, an "amorphous institutionalized power . . . which suggests neither nature nor people,"[9] for in it responsibility is no longer central to communal life but is instead a part of the legal system. Thus Sula's interaction with the community, her neighborhood, from which she is alienated, is of paramount importance.

Sula's status as outsider manifests itself symbolically in a mysterious birthmark that runs from the middle of the lid toward the eyebrow of her right eye. It marks her as evil to most Bottomites, who blame her for unpleasant occurrences. For example, when Teapot knocks on Sula's door to ask for empty bottles, he falls off the porch while leaving. His mother accuses Sula of pushing him. When Mr. Finley dies, Sula is blamed. He was sitting on his porch sucking chicken bones, as he had done for thirteen years, when he saw Sula and choked.

Her peripheral life makes Sula a scapegoat for the Bottom's citizens. Philip Royster contends, "the folk create the scapegoat by identifying Sula as the cause of the misery, which they identify as evil, in their lives. It is undoubtedly easier for the folk to anthropomorphize their misery than to examine the generation of that misery by their relation to the environment. The folk produced good in their lives, that is, loving and caring for one another, by reacting to their own conception of evil, Sula, who they considered a witch."[10] From the outset, Sula's role as scapegoat is clearly established. The community's "conviction of

Sula's evil changed them in accountable yet mysterious ways. Once the
source of their personal misfortune was identified, they had to leave to
protect and love one another. They began to cherish their husbands and
wives, protect children, repair their homes and in general band together against the devil in their midst" (117–18).

What Banyiwa-Horne suggests is of paramount importance. Sula,
she argues, "becomes a pariah precisely because she rejects those values
that aim at uniformity and stifle the self."[11] Her willingness to reject
them makes her "evil" to those in the community who never express
their own "freedom of the will." Sula is "evil" because she, unlike Nel
for example, does not live "totally by the law" nor surrender "completely to it without questioning anything sometimes"; she is "perfectly
willing to think the unthinkable."[12]

Directly speaking, Sula's rebelliousness manifests itself in several
ways. Unlike other Medallion women, including Nel, Sula refuses to
marry, settle down, and raise a family. Moreover, as insult to them she
attends their church functions underwearless, buys and picks over their
food, and "tries out" and discards their husbands. She feels no obligation to please anyone unless she in turn gains pleasure. As she once
confessed to Nel: "I got my mind. And what goes on in it" (43). Her
determination to achieve self-fulfillment allows her to "live in the
world" (43), but not be caught up in the spiderweb-like life of the
Bottom where she would be called upon to conform, to "dangle in dry
places suspended by [her] own spittle more terrified of the free fall than
the snake's breath below" (103–104).

At issue is the whole question of "good and evil," for if Nel Wright is
positive (her names suggest as much), then Sula is the opposite. Yet
Morrison does not assess this age-old concern in strictly religious,
particularly Christian, terms. In Morrisonian discourse, evil is not a sin
against God, per se. Conceptually, it is inverted to become a sin against
oneself; it is one's failure to act existentially. Though Sula is viewed as
evil, in the final analysis it is the Bottom's women, who do not "protest
God's will but acknowledge it and confirm . . . their conviction that
the only way to avoid the Hand of God is to get in it" (66), who emerge
as less attractive. They sit passively during the eulogy for Chicken
Little with unfolded hands, "like pairs of raven's wings" (65), suggesting a sense of total helplessness. What is significant, however, is that
the Bottom community does not move to destroy or eradicate Sula from
its midst. It tolerates her. Morrison explains that for blacks, "Evil is
not an alien force; it's just a different force."[13] In spite of her noncon-

formist behavior, Sula is tolerated until she commits the unpardonable sin of putting her grandmother in an old folks home. This is out of sync with the notion of "neighborhood"—the extended compound where people care for and look after one another.

Paradoxically, for many critics, Morrison falls victim to traditional stereotypes in her treatment of Sula and the blacks of the Bottom. As noted earlier, Gayle sees her characters as "primitives." While Odette Martin believes *Sula* "breathes new life" into traditional Black stereotypes—with Eva as "the folk woman," Hannah as the "primitive," Cecile Sabat as the "tragic mulatto," and Sula as the "exotic"—he associates these images with the romanticism of a *"Negritude* tradition," which he believes Morrison sets out to criticize. Martin concludes: "It is difficult to perceive that repeating images, even for critical purposes, is to provide them with certain legitimacy."[14]

In the end what might be true, however, is suggested by Barbara Lounsberry and Grace Ann Hovet, who argue that Morrison is more interested in showing "the constriction and ultimate futility of any single ordering vision [traditional institutions such as church, family, state] within the black community."[15] A desire to transcend the sterile soil of the Bottom, coupled with her need for independence, lead Sula away from it. After years of traveling and pursuing an education, she returns, having discovered that the Bottom and Medallion are microcosmic of the world at large. They are thus as appropriate as anywhere else for her pursuit of self.

The Peace Women

The verbal exchange Sula has with her grandmother Eva upon returning to Medallion evolves around the impact the Peace women have on their progeny in her quest for authentic existence. In the midst of the conversation Eve asks:

> "When you gone to get married? You need to have babies. It'll settle you."
> "I don't want to make somebody else. I want to make myself."
> "Selfish. Ain't no woman got no business floatin' around without no man." (79–80)

On the one hand, Sula's existential pronouncement—"I want to make myself"—is in character, because it is the adult voice, the voice of Sula-as-woman, that we hear. Eva's defense of the traditional roles of women, on the other hand, might seem out of place at first, especially because her name suggests that she is at one (at peace) with herself and because her sense of wholeness does not center on traditional views of women as only wives and mothers. Thus, as Martin notes, "Sula is to be taken as a model for Black womanhood insofar as she chooses to define herself, as opposed to telling culture to do so, especially since its definitions are negative ones."[16]

During Sula's childhood, it appears that neither Eva nor Hannah served as a positive role model who enforced or exhibited a lifestyle of domestic tranquility or security. In fact, just the opposite appears true, for neither woman provided Sula with an "intimate knowledge of marriage" (103). In the Peace house the women behaved like "all men [were] available," and so they "selected from among them with a care only for their taste" (103). Contrary to Chikwenye Okonjo Ogunyemi, however, they are not whores, like the prostitutes in *The Bluest Eye*.[17] Their interest in men has to do with pleasure, not economics and pure hate. In fact, Eva and Hannah conformed to convention by marrying and raising families.

Their traditional behavior ends there, however. For example, although she was once married, Hannah never bothers to remarry after being left a widow. She gives Sula an unconventional image of womanhood and motherhood through her "sooty" lifestyle. "Hannah simply refused to live without the attentions of a man, after Rekus's death she had a steady sequence of lovers, mostly the husbands of her friends and neighbors" (36). Moreover, in her mother/daughter role, Hannah, who had not found Eva to be a loving mother, comes up short on the nurturing yardstick. She damages Sula's childhood by confessing that although she had the obligatory love of a parent for her child, she "just don't like her" (49). From her mother Sula would learn that "sex was pleasant and frequent, but otherwise unremarkable" (37–38). Consequently, Sula's lack of desire for domestic ties seems a natural legacy, for like the other Peace women, she "simply loved maleness, for its own sake" (41). Hannah's remark, however, will have the most lasting impact and lead Sulla to the independence she strives for with her "experimental life" (102). Indirectly, Hannah has taught Sula that "there was no other [than self] that [one] could count on" (102).

That Sula has no feelings of self-disparagement must be attributed in part to her grandmother, Eva, as well. It is Eva's influence on the young Sula that leads her to accept the code of ethics practiced in the Peace home, disallowing any guilt over licentiousness or hint of inferiority, even though the community on the whole regards the Peace women as not merely unethical but socially unacceptable. Bottomites, such as Helene Wright, expected Sula to have her "mother's slackness" (29); they are surprised to discover that she does not. When she meets Sula for the first time, "Helene's curdled scorn turned to butter" (29). Consequently, as Martin asserts, "While Sula's relationships function as an explicit criticism of Black values and patterns of behavior, they are also a vehicle for grasping Sula's real identity. She is neither evil nor a fixed, unchanging Absolute. Rather, as the sensual and the experimental, she represents potential: the raw energy of Life and the creative impulse of Art."[18]

Such assesssment does not take into account the question of accountability, which is Cynthia Dubin Edelberg's central argument when she questions the assertions Morrison makes relating to formal education, the work ethic, and the Bible through the untrammelled characters in her "brutal fictional world."[19] According to Edelberg, "the narrator in Morrison's novels does not permit the characters to succeed through channels generally thought to be useful and reliable." Specifically, in *Sula,* Edelberg maintains, "formal education is derided, characters with Biblical names live their namesakes' lives in reverse, and the omniscient narrator will not allow the all pervasive suffering to come to rest."[20]

Edelberg offers a purely literal reading of *Sula,* making it a "grotesque though essentially realistic novel." Consequently, she overlooks the central ironies and contradictions of the text, as well as Morrison's propensity to topsy-turvy the norm for the sake of emphasis and exploration. Although it is true that Sula "ridicules" education as one of the conventional ways that blacks have transcended their otherwise circumscribed lives, she does take the pain to achieve formal training by going to college. Moreover, Morrison is an academic who, no matter what her connection with the world of letters as a writer or editor, continues to teach, lecture, visit, and assume residencies on college and university campuses across the United States, suggesting not only a belief in the value of these institutions and the educational process but, perhaps most important, a commitment to them. Her children, too, are being formally educated. Above all, however, it would be most contradictory for Morrison to create someone interested in her "Me-ness" and have that character defer self to a process that is often either restrictive or alienating. Consequently, Sula's rejection of formal education is in character. She is not about saving the race but herself.

More important, Edelberg overlooks the fact that Eva and Hannah

provide the community of women that nurtures Sula, directly and
indirectly, allowing her to see the alternatives available to her, as
woman, wife, and mother. Although she questions traditional use (and
misuse) of Christianity, Morrison seems more interested in examining
the full implications of her characters' biblical names rather than in
revealing the Bible as "the wrong book," as Edelberg also suggests.[21]

Eva (Eve) provides the ideal, for she is the archetypal "Great
Mother." She is the numinous woman who embodies the feminine
principle and, consequently, fulfills rather than mocks her name, as
Edelberg suggests. Abandoned without a means of support by her
husband, Boy Boy, Eva is forced to become self-sufficient and provide
for herself and three children. Destitution forces her to leave them in a
neighbor's care for eighteen months. When she returns, she has only
one leg, but she has the economic wherewithal to support her family.
Isolating herself in a room on the top of her home, Eva supervises the
activities within, seldom descending to the lower level.

As the Great Mother, Eva nourishes and protects her family, providing sustenance and life. She reveals that meeting her children's needs is
her primary concern when Hannah, who equates love with play, asks
Eva about her love for her children. Eva explains that she never had
time for recreation: "No time. They wasn't no time. Not none. Soon as
I got one day done here comes a night. With you all coughin' and me
watchin' so TB wouldn't take you off and if you was sleepin' quiet I
thought O Lord, they dead and put my hand over your mouth to feel if
the breadth was comin' what you talk' 'bout did I love you girl I stayed
alive for you can't you get that through your thick head" (60).

Eva's role as Great Mother is further exemplified in her efforts to
save Hannah, her firstborn. Hannah has a prophetic dream in which
she attends a wedding in a red dress; she later burns to death in spite
of Eva's fervent attempt to save her. Seeing her daughter's dress on
fire,

Eva knew there was time for nothing in this world than the time it took to get
there and cover her daughter's body with her own. She lifted her heavy frame
up on her good leg, and with fists and arms smashed the windowpane. Using
her stump as a support on the window sill, her good leg as lever, she threw
herself out the window. Cut and bleeding she clawed the air trying to aim her
body toward the flaming, dancing figure. She missed and came crashing down
some twelve feet from Hannah's smoke. Stunned but still conscious, Eva
dragged herself toward her firstborn. (65)

The emphasis here is strictly on the sacrificial role woman-as-mother is often called upon to assumed, a role Morrison will explore in depth in *Beloved*.

Eva is also seen in this role in her more successful effort to save Plum, her youngest child and only son. When constipation threatened his life in infancy, she unclogs his bowels with fingers lubricated with lard, "the last bit of food she had in the world. . . . And now that it was over, Eva squatted there [in the outhouse in the middle of a cold winter's night] to free his stool, and what was she doing down on her haunches with her beloved baby boy warmed by her body in the almost darkness, her shins and teeth freezing, her nostrils assailed" (34). That motherhood calls for sacrifices is clearly the point being made.

Although her role as Great Mother places Eva in a situation that requires her to sacrifice, if necessary, her life for her children's, Eva, as a complete sign of this archetype, must embody the dark side of this role as well. Consequently, she is also cast in the role of "Terrible Mother." Eva, like Eve, is inescapably the taker of life as well as the giver of life. She is, in other words, capable of devouring and destroying that which she has given life. She sacrifices herself, but she is also able to sacrifice her son, if and when necessary, as in the Adonisian myth.[22]

When Plum returns from the war (which makes him a warrior, like Adonis) mired in heroine addiction, Eva is not able to accept his self-destructive behavior, slovenliness, and diminishment to a mere shadow of himself. She takes away his life by engulfing him in fire, while he lays embraced in the warm thought of her love and the false sense of security induced by his narcotic state.

In what we at first perceive as a merciless, inhuman act, we find, although in exaggerated form, a lesson in the ultimate importance of the self-reliance that Sula must come to realize and accept. Scarred, too, like Shadrack, Plum seeks to escape independence through drugs rather than to act responsibly to establish an order and chart a direction for his fragmented life. His infantile behavior is a metaphor for lack of independence. He wanted to return to the womb, Eva explains, suggesting an act of "Bad Faith" on his part. "He wanted to crawl back into my womb. I ain't got the room no more even if he could do it. . . . And he was crawlin' back, being helpless and thinking baby thoughts and dreaming baby dreams and messing up his pants again and smiling all the time" (62).

As Eva suggests, what Plum sought was not incestuous cohabitation, but escape through rebirth and childhood. He wanted to become a child again, to return to the parental shelter she once offered, to avoid responsibility for self, as well as to be restored and made new. Unable to accept either her son's dependence or his inevitable decay, Eva destroys him. As she reminds Hannah, however, her love for Plum had not abated. She tells her: "I held him close first. Real close. Sweet Plum. My baby boy" (62).

Through Morrison's careful use of tropes throughout the passage we are able to find embedded in the text an excellent use of mythology, for Plum's burning might also be viewed as an act of purgation—a rite of purification. The language here is filled with images and symbols of cleansing, renewal, and rebirth: "Plum on the rim of a warm light sleep . . . He felt twilight. Now there seemed to be some kind of wet light traveling over his legs and stomach with a deep attractive smell. It wound itself—this wet light—all about him, splashing and running into his skin. He opened his eyes and saw what he imagined was the great wing of an eagle pouring a wet lightness over him. Some kind of baptism, some kind of blessing, he thought" (47). The images of wetness and light recall the embryonal fluid of the uterus, and the reference to "twilight" signifies rebirth, the dawning of a new day. That his will be a more spiritual rebirth than a physical one is suggested by the eagle and the "wet lightness" that it pours over Plum. Ironically, then, Plum's death symbolically leads to new life, in the final analysis. In the dominant images of the warm fire and secure bed, we find semblances of the nurturing womb. Eva, in spite of her pronouncements, provides rebirth for her defiled son, suggesting why he remains her "baby boy."

The passage resonates, on the one hand, with the traditional African's concept of *eschatology,* or afterlife. Death is perceived as a significant phase in a movement that includes birth, life, death, and rebirth that evolves from the African's cyclical concept of time. Thus, the notion of a world of the "living dead" (a community of the departed) is prevalent in traditional African cosmology; here individuals are dead in body but not in spirit, especially if they are remembered by the surviving members of their family who remain in commune with him or her.[23] Although death is a major theme in *Sula,* it, like the notion of evil, is not pursued strictly in the Western sense. Morrison explores such primordial human concerns from an Afro-centric perspective to illustrate the multifaceted responses of black life.

We must note, however, that her angle of vision is not limited to the Afro-centric alone; Plum's burning also recalls Western mythologies of death and rebirth. This is most evident in the "deep attractive smell" and "great wing of an eagle" and in the reference to Plum's dirgelike lullaby and the comparison of Eva's movements with those of a heron. Together, they recall the purple-colored (note the significant use of the name Plum) phoenix (and its prototypes as the heron and eagle), whose power lies in its ability to die and resurrect itself.

Building its nest with the sweetest spices (Eva sees that Plum has been drinking what she thinks is a glass of strawberry crush soda), the phoenix sits, singing its sweetest song (we hear this in his chuckles and Eva's lullaby), while its nest, ignited by the sun's ray (fire) is transformed into a pyre. From the ashes, a new phoenix emerges to transport the remains of its parents to Heliopole, the City of the Sun, for burial. Thus, this myth is often associated with the solar journey, which includes distinct phases of birth (sunrise), death (sunset), and rebirth (sunrise); phases that remain paramount to Eva's son (sun).

With this apparent allusion to the mythical phoenix and to traditional African cosmology, Morrison continues and in fact crystallizes the tropes and themes that will recur from this point on in her collected works, demonstrating not only her willingness to borrow from traditional myths but also to weave her own by merging Western, African, and African-American folk beliefs, mythologies, mysticism, and magic. For example, we find her placing at the center of her literary cosmology traditional notions of the significance of the elements: earth, air, water, fire. We saw them in *The Bluest Eye* in the failure of the seeds to grow in the earth.

Water images, prevalent in *Sula,* are for the most part associated with death, as with Chicken Little and the Bottomites who plunge to their death in the cave. But it is also *aqua vitae,* as in the case of Shardrack, whose vocation and avocation as a fisherman are intertwined with life. Fire, though associated with death, as in the case of Hannah, is also a form of ritual cleansing, and we see this with both Shadrack and Plum. Significant, too, are the natural cycles, such as the solar movement, which in *Sula* is associated with maleness; lunar cycles will be associated with females in later works. We find significant explorations of the role of womanhood and motherhood, of woman-as-woman, wife, and perhaps more important, as mother—a role that will be associated more with nurturing and nursing (with the mother's milk) than with the mere act of giving birth to children. Most important, however, is the fact that the meanings of these myths are approached from a black woman's point of view.

Thus, one might conclude that in Morrison's canon biblical myths are not necessarily debunked as much as they are expanded. We find ample evidence of this in Eva, who lives up to her name. Like the biblical Eve, she is the mother of life, "of all living things." This explains the presence of so many different kinds of people living in her home as well as Eva's power to name and classify, visible in her treatment of the Deweys. Morrison expands Eva's character, forcing us to realize that Eva cannot be romanticized for her more benevolent qualities alone. Lighter and darker sides add to her complexity and credibility. She must simultaneously be the mother of Life and Death. Even in biblical mythology Death entered the world when Eve sinned, a point that Edelberg misses.

More important, however, is the fact that with Eva we have the ideal image of total self-reliance. Eva willingly makes choices. It is not coincidental that in treatment and characterization she emerges as a goddess, as builder and ruler of her own house. *She* builds and rules her dominion at 7 Carpenter's Road, which both in name and number suggests a creative act—the power of self-creation that one would associate with the divine power of a goddess (God created His world in seven days). She is "creator and sovereign" (26), and we see the world from her perspective.

Sula inherits as legacy from her community of women arrogance and self-indulgence: "Eva's and Hannah's self-indulgence merged in her and, with a twist that was all her own imagination, she lived out her days exploring her own thoughts and emotions, giving them full reign, feeling no obligation to please anybody unless their pleasure pleased her. As willing to feel pain as to give pain, to feel pleasure, hers was an experimental life" (102). It is thus not surprising that as an adult Sula "went to bed with men as frequently as she could" (105), but it is also unsurprising that she rebelled against the traditional role of woman as wife and mother that her untraditional parents indirectly, if not directly, encouraged her to follow. Her promiscuity, however, must be considered an essential aspect of her "experimental life," her independence and self-reliance, not solely as a desire to be amoral.

Thus, in the Peace women—Eva, Hannah, and Sula—we find the creative act of inversion, of topsy-turvydom, that becomes a positive, creative force in the lives of Morrison's characters. Indeed, they act and feel good about their lives when they sabotage the status quo. In the final analysis, Morrison's Sula is warm, subjective, uninhibited, and irrational. She is a free spirit who is not bound by external mores and values. She declared to Nel:

". . . Me, I'm going down like one of those redwoods. I sure did live in this world."

"Really?" What have you go to show for it?"

"Show?" To who? Girl, I got my mind. And what goes on in it. Which is to say, I got me."

"Lonely, ain't it?"

"Yes. But my lonely is *mine*." (123)

Here, Sula clearly suggests that, unlike Pecola, she is accountable to no one but herself for the direction of her life. Her determination to assume existential responsibility for self is indicated by her vociferous declaration: "I got my mind," the creative assertion that wills what one wishes. This act, indeed, given their histories, could not be expected from the Breedlove family.

In the end, however, Sula's untrammelled spirit remains problematic, for she seems to lack interest in assuming any responsibility for her fellow human beings. This apparent lack may explain why she dies so early in the novel, although she is never outrightly expelled by the community. Barbara Christian concludes that "Morrison resists the idea that either individual pursuit or community conservatism is enough for fulfillment. Left without a context, the self has 'no speck from which to grow' (103), and deprived of creative spirits, the community succumbs to death and destruction."[24]

Nel Wright

In the midst of Sula's chaotic youth, one constant remained to provide sanctuary: Nel, who throughout their childhood together, had been a complementary force. For Sula, Nel became a confidante, a source of security, especially after Sula overheard Hannah's remarks about love and like. Their friendship became so close that they "themselves had difficulty distinguishing one's thought from the other" (72).

Yet it must be argued that their relationship was not simply one of being-for-the-other; for there was reciprocity, although ironically during their childhood it was Nel who led and Sula who followed: "They were solitary little girls whose loneliness was so profound it intoxicated them and sent them stumbling into Technicolored visions that always included a presence, a someone, who, quite like the dreamer, shared the delight of the dream" (44).

During their childhood Nel and Sula were "daughters of distant mothers and incomprehensible fathers" (44). Conformity, making things right (as her name "Wright" suggests), was the operative word in Nel's home. In her effort to escape her past, which included a prostitute mother, Helene, Nel's mother, "saw more comfort and purpose than she had ever hoped to find in this life" (15) through her daughter. Consequently, she reared her daughter on principles of obedience and politeness: "Any enthusiasm that little Nel showed was calmed by the mother until she drove her daughter's imagination underground" (16).

Nel recaptures her sense of self and aborts the role her properly behaved mother had identified for her when, after a trip down South, she discovers her mother's frailty and fears. "I am me," she whispers. "Me. . . . I'm me. I'm not their daughter. I'm not Nel. I'm me. Me" (24). This self-reclamation, this certainty of identity, becomes a creative act that makes Nel self-reliant. Nel's confidence and Sula's insecurity formed the foundation of the reciprocity that characterized their friendship, providing them with the most important relationship in their lives. For Sula, Nel was "the other half of her equation" (105); together they formed a whole. "They found relief in each other's personality" (45). By the time they reach adulthood, however, the tables turn. Sula displays a desire to live outside the norm, to lead rather than to follow. Nel, on the other hand, succumbs to the expected and becomes a wife and mother through her marriage to Jude Green.

Sula's unconventional standards and life-style, coupled with the fact that as girls she and Nel had "never quarreled . . . the way some girlfriends did over boys or competed against each other for them" (72), lead Sula to bed with Nel's husband, after she returns to Medallion. But Sula and Nel are no longer adolescents, and Sula's action serves only to destroy the friendship—the most meaningful experience she had known. Although she had considered Nel "the closest thing to both an other and a self" (103), she discovers that "she and Nel were not one and the same thing" (103). In the end, then, Sula's return is not to the community—that is, to traditional values, for these are counterproductive in her view. She returns to a friendship, which, paradoxically, she destroys.

In her unconventional view of life, Sula makes a distinction between sex and friendship—a view that Nel, in her conventionality, does not share. For Sula, sex, though "pleasant and frequent," is "unremark-able," unlike her remarkable friendship with Nel. Admitting to Nel that they were "good friends," Sula, years later, is unable to see the wrong she committed. She tells Nel: "What you mean take him away? I didn't kill him, I just fucked him. If we were such good friends, how come you couldn't get over it" (125).

Nel's marriage to Jude, however, had given her an identity that required her to forfeit the necessary sense of self that remains salient to Sula. Because Jude's subsequent departure left Nel with "thighs [that] were really empty" (95), as Byerman correctly notes, "the loss of Jude is the loss of identity and the loss of life. . . . [Nel] now becomes 'a woman without a man' and unable to raise her eyes. For this change she blames Sula, who, without a sense of ownership, cannot conceive of Jude as an object to be taken."[25]

What is important for Sula is the friendship she had nurtured and developed with Nel in the midst of a world that promised fragmenta-tion. Emphasis is placed on their having been "girls *together*." It is their togetherness—their friendship together—that led to their sense of indi-vidualism. Ironically, the significance of their togetherness is what Nel, who thought she had missed Jude all along, realizes in the end. It is the multifaceted signification of being "girls together"—and above all its loss—that is echoed in Nel's excruciating declaration: "We was girls together . . . O Lord, Sula . . . girl, girl, girlgirlgirl" (149).

Morrison is definite and calculating in her presentation of the depth of friendship between black women. In a conversation with Claudia Tate, she confesses to wanting to write about such friendship: "When I wrote *Sula,* I knew I was going to write a book about good and evil and about friendship. Seemed to me that black women have friends in the old-fashioned sense of the word."[26]

By providing Sula and Nel with the secret of Chicken Little's acciden-tal death, and specifically by having Nel provide the strength and support Sula needed at the moment, Morrison further united them in a manner that would bond them for eternity. Although the action was Sula's, the involvement, as Eva would later point out, was clearly theirs together. After all, Nel suggests the cover-up when she tells Sula, *"Let's go. We can't bring him back"* (146). Eva is thus correct when years later she questions Nel:

"Tell me how you killed that little boy?"
"What? What little boy?"
"The one you threw in the water . . ."
"I didn't throw no little boy in the river. That was Sula."
"You. Sula. What's the difference?"
". . . Never was no difference between you." (144–145)

In the end, then, Sula and Nel are vital parts of the same personality.
Together they form a whole, in spite of their differences. According to
Morrison, although Nel has limitations and lacks Sula's imagination,
"they are very much alike. They complement each other. They support
each other."[27]

Men in *Sula*

That this unique level of friendship generally does not exist between
men and women is suggested in Morrison's treatment of male-female
relationships. For the most part, the men in *Sula* are superficial, immature, untrustworthy, and anonymous, as is suggested by their names
Jude (Judas), Green (naive), Boy-Boy (infantile), Chicken Little (fearful
and diminutive), the Deweys (anonymous), and so forth. The negative
aspects of their names are most visible when juxtaposed with the em-
powering names of the women. The men's behavior, for the most part,
is less than heroic—even Ajax's, whose name is obviously borrowed
from a Greek warrior. Each leaves a community of abandoned women.
This abandonment becomes the impetus for Eva, the paradigmatic
woman who must rebound through assertiveness and self-reliance or be
lost, after she and her children are deserted by her husband/their father.
She does rebound through the powerful symbolic act of building her
own house, establishing her own territory, the sanctum of her mind
(consciousness), "sixty feet from Boy-Boy's one-room cabin" (30).

Thus Eva's domicile is more than a "ramshackle house" with boarders
and stray beings, as some critics argue. There would be no "men in the
house, no men to run it" (35). It is not uncommon for critics to claim
that the male-female relationships in *Sula* are often marked by mental
and physical violence. Hovet and Lounsberry do not offer such a simplistic view, but instead propose more complex courses that may explain
the tension in these relationships, including the provocative one that
"the 'diminishment' of the black male may be caused by excessive
'mothering,' by both black wives and mother, as well as by social
discrimination."[28]

Even self-willed Sula becomes a victim when, in her pivotal and at first nontraditionanl relationship with Ajax, she goes against the lessons her grandmother taught her and even her own personal convictions. The results are fatal. At first, the relationship provides not only physical and sexual completion but also what seems like spiritual wholeness in the form of love. Sula is attracted to him because of "his refusal to baby or protect her, his assumption that she was both tough and wise" (10). He is attracted to her because "[h]er elusiveness and indifference to establish habits of behavior reminded him of his mother," (109) "an evil conjure woman" (109). Unlike her previous relationships, this one gives her "real pleasure," from a gift bearer who showers her with butterflies, wild berries, stolen bottles of milk, and "meal fried porgies wrapped in a salmon colored sheet of the *Pittsburgh Courier*" (108). At first, reciprocity is the operative word in their relationship. And indeed this should be expected because they consummate their relationship in Eva's house, where individualism formed the foundation. Moreover, Ajax not only speaks to her but also listens and recognizes her brilliance. Assuming that she is tough and wise, he shuns chauvinism and refuses paternalism. She dominates him at times, and in their lovemaking she has an equal share as a contributing partner.

In the metamorphosis that occurs in their relationship, however, Sula confuses love with possession. She transforms Eva's house into a domestic haven where "the bathroom was gleaming, the bed was made and the table was set for two" (113). Perhaps the ultimate indications of change, however, are the green ribbons that she places in her hair and her invitation that Ajax become dependent upon her: "Come on. Lean on me" (115). Ajax, a would-be pilot, abruptly walks out of her life, leaving her "with nothing but stunning absence" (115). The depth of the consequence of Sula's deferment of self becomes apparent when she later discovers that she does not even know his correct name: Albert Jacks. She concludes: "if I didn't know his name, then there is nothing I did know and I have known nothing ever at all" (117). Sula seems here to learn the lessons Pecola's life had served to teach. Having sought authenticity and verification externally, that is, from her relationship with others, she had become vulnerable to the dictates of others, which led to a greater sense of liminality and invisibility. Failing to continue her course of self-definition by aborting her heretofore uncompromising values, Sula is no longer self-reliant. This, too, brings on her death, which, much like Pecola's insanity, is inevitable.

Shadrack

Shadrack, the Bottom's jester/fisherman, is more successful in maintaining an authentic self. Through him, Morrison explores the experiences of a person who is in the midst of individuation, a process that, according to Swiss psychiatrist Carl Jung, involves becoming "a single homogeneous being, becoming the unique person that one in fact is."[29] Indeed, Shadrack, like the Bottomites, is interested in finding out what he is about, is involved in a quest for psychological wholeness.

Before coming to the Bottom, Shadrack had spent a year in a mental institution, where he had been placed after his brutalizing World War I experience left him physically and psychologically handicapped. After witnessing the death of a fellow soldier in an explosion that he survives, Shadrack, like his biblical namesake, emerges from the conflagration. Here, too, we find the image of the phoenix. He is nevertheless scarred by his encounter with death. A neurotic who believes that his hands have grown to monstrous proportions, Shadrack has no sense of who or what he is. Left practically in a state of tabula rasa, or blankness, he remains unbalanced and suffers from having "no past, no language, no tribe, no source, no address book, no comb, no pencil, no clock, no pocket handkerchief, no rug, no bed, no can opener, no faded postcard, no soap, no key, no tobacco pouch, no soiled underwear and nothing nothing nothing to do" (10). As Ogunyemi explains, Shadrack's "apparent madness is Morrison's cynical commentary on a world gone awry . . . Shadrack somehow survives the fire of war but remains a ghost of his former self."[30]

That Shadrack is faced with fragmentation is indicated by his desire to tie together "the loose cords in his mind" (8). Unable to do so immediately, during a moment of cogitation, he allows his mind "to slip into whatever cave mouths of memory it chose" (8). During the ensuing dream, he sees a "window that looked out on a river which he knew was full of fish [and] someone was speaking softly just outside the door" (8). Considering this dream a roadmap to his identity, Shadrack sets out to find, upon his release from the institution, the setting he had envisioned. He finds it in Medallion, his former home, which was only twenty-two miles away.

In her development and treatment of Shadrack's effort to cement the "loose cords" in his mind, Morrison establishes a pattern of action that parallels Jungian ideas related to the definition and function of the psyche and its fundamental components: the self, ego, shadow, anima (female) and animus (male). Most important, she uses Jung's concepts of the conscious and the unconscious selves, which function in a compensatory manner to maintain an ordering and unifying center of the total psyche. Using dreams (and particularly "Big Dreams") as vehicles, the "Collective Unconscious," whose contents include "all future things that are taking in shape in [the individual] and will sometime come to Consciousness,"[31] is continuously engaged in dramatization, Jung argued, which leads to a harmonious relationship between it and the conscious mind. Its archetypes or spontaneous symbols provide the pieces to the puzzle that the individual needs to complete the self.

It is within the realm of the dramatization that the significance of Shadrack's experience during his institutionalization can be best understood. For it is the workings of his collective unconscious, grouping and regrouping its contents in an effort to strike a balance with its conscious mind, that provide Shadrack with the dream and specific images and symbols that, when understood by his conscious mind, set him on the path to transformation and rebirth that result in actualization and wholeness. As we learn from the narrator, Shadrack's mind slips into whatever "cave mouths of memory it chooses." What the narrator suggests here is that Shadrack's mind is reacting to his experience in such a way that indelible memory patterns can be produced. From this involuntary process, Shadrack is able to secure relevant data that will assist him in striking the balance he desperately needs and seeks.

That Shadrack plunges into the depth of his collective unconscious in search of self is suggested by Morrison's careful use of language and tropes. Such words as *memory* and *cave* can be taken as symbols of the unconscious. Whereas memory is often associated with a place in the unconscious where time and space emerge, of temporary subliminal content, cave is a common symbol for the unconscious itself. Also important are the images Shadrack sees: the window and the river. Although it would vary from individual to individual in Jungian analysis, the window might very well symbolize the conscious, that which looks out or is outwardly seen. The river, a body of water, is the commonest symbol of the collective unconscious. Shadrack's dream, then, one might assume, means that he is on a path of seeking harmony between the two important components of the self: the conscious and unconscious, with this descent into the collective unconscious. For Morrison, this would be termed the act of *re-memory*.

Dreams are not only compensatory but also, for Jung, prospective or anticipatory: through them the unconscious anticipates future conscious achievements and offers them to the conscious in sketches (rough drafts). Thus, Shadrack's dream might be taken to represent not only his search for psychological wholeness but also a luminous moment that reveals the very vehicle he needs to achieve it. In the final analysis, he realizes that he has a place where the window, river, and voices are. By descending into the unconscious through his dream, Shadrack is able to emerge—to ascend—experience rebirth from a fragmented life and begin to find tangible meaning and order.

Assured of some tangible direction for his life, Shadrack sets out on a journey to self, which not coincidentally is one that he has been involved in all his life: at twenty-two years of age he is twenty-two miles from the setting of his dream, Medallion, the self. As a final indication of his determination to find and accept this self, Shadrack, while briefly incarcerated, forces himself to confront it by looking at his reflection in the toilet bowl in his cell: "There in the toilet water he saw a grave black face. A black so definite, so unequivocal, it admonished him. He had been harboring a skittish apprehension that he was not real—that he didn't exist at all. But when the blackness greeted him with its indisputable presence, he wanted nothing more" (11).

In this symbolic act of self-reflection, Shadrack, at this stage fundamentally devoid of ego and persona, sees his true self in yet another symbolic descent into the unconscious. But in contrast to his dream, which is involuntary, his action here, which involves a confrontation of his physical self, is willful. Significantly, he sees a self that is tied to race, the missing, tangible element that must be restored if the whole self—psychological and physical—is to emerge. In the end, then, it is his lost personal history that he desperately needs to tie the loose ends in his mind. He, like Sula, but unlike Pecola, chooses to accept who he is historically rather than try to escape from it.

Accepting the blackness that greets him becomes a creative, existential act that leads Shadrack toward an authentic existence. It provides him with an umbilical attachment to history, collective and personal, and consequently to the needed grounding available to him in Medallion alone, which we may now clearly see as not only a metaphor for his created self but also, given what we know about the Bottom and its residents, a self that embodies the African-American experience. The toilet bowl and cell thus become tropes for his legacy of oppression and suffering. Ironically, they are nurturing wombs (water is the crucial element), from which his ultimate rebirth will take place.

To reach the desired level of authenticity, however, Shadrack must transcend the one remaining impediment: his fear of death and dying. To do so, he founds National Suicide Day on which to confront both and thus affix some order to his life. Finally achieving a desired level of self-affirmation, Shadrack behaves in a manner revelatory of a totally self-derived and -controlled individual. Like Sula, he spurns social prescriptions. He walks about with his penis exposed, urinates in front of ladies and girls, curses white people, drinks in the street from the mouth of the bottle, and shouts and shakes in the street.

His unconventional behavior alienates him from the Bottom community, which considers him a lunatic. He lives, literally and figuratively, on the outskirts of the Bottom, suggesting, like Sula's birthmark, his status as pariah, as outsider. What seems true, however, is that his encounter with his deeper unconscious self integrates his anima side, freeing him from the binding effects of the ego, leaving him unsaddled by inhibitions, fears, hopes, and the ambitions (values) of those around him. And perhaps more important, it allows him to turn his world topsy-turvy. Because he is not being ego centered and is controlled to some degree by his "shadow," or darker side, as his name clearly suggests, Shadrack has to be viewed as immoral or amoral by those who become "the Other," although for him these values are the embodiment of authentic existence and creativity.

Yet Morrison does not suggest through her characterization of Shadrack that he should function as a role model in the Bottom for others. Shadrack carries no symbol of power or authority akin to Eva's scepter-like crutches; nor does he demand that others conform to a life like his. He is, in the final analysis, prophet-as-doer/actor—who, as his biblical name implies, determines the direction of his own life, regardless of the outcome—rather than prophet-as-speaker/leader, who dictates the actions of others.

This is true even of his action each 3 January. Although his ritual on National Suicide Day has become "part of the fabric of life up in the Bottom," his is a "solitary parade" (13), in which he converts the Bottom into a ritual ground for his own rite of cleansing and rejuvenation. When the generally passive Bottomites decide to follow Shadrack in "a pied piper's band" (137), they plunge to their deaths. Ironically, as the narrator tells us, "They knew Shadrack was crazy but that did not mean that he didn't have any sense or, even more important, that he had no power" (12). But his power is over self. This reminds us of what Morrison tells Claudia Tate, "If you own yourself, you can make some types of choices, take certain kinds of risks."[33] It is not coincidental that he survives.

It is also unsurprising that the only person to gain insight into Shadrack's complexity is Sula. Like him, she occupies a position as communal scapegoat and pariah. Sula affirms their bond and establishes an intuitive relation with Shadrack when, after accidentally drowning a playmate, she goes to Shadrack's cabin to confirm what, if anything, he has witnessed. She is immediately startled by the contrast between the externally chaotic and disarrayed Shadrack and the neatness and order, the restfulness, peacefulness, and secure quality of his simple abode, a symbol of the degree of wholeness he possesses. She thinks, "Perhaps this was not the house of Shad . . . With its made-bed? With its rag rug and wooden table?" (53). When Shadrack arrives to find her there, he welcomes his only visitor ever with a simple "Always," an apparent answer to an unspoken question.

His answer may allude to a question of the permanence of life, or so he would have us believe. It could, however, express the opposite, which he would later discover to be true: death is the only given in life. It alone will "always" endure, as years later the incident on New River Road would further suggest. Ironically, those who had gone down into the watery grave were attempting to destroy vicariously (undoubtedly now too late) those who in killing their dreams had relegated them to a life deferred. They ended up killing themselves, now physically rather than merely symbolically as in the past.

In the end Shadrack's "always" must also refer to the single most important act of adhering "always" to one's personal convictions. Paradoxically, Sula takes flight, totally unaware of not only the importance of this lesson but the complexity of its implications, as her life with Ajax would eventually bear out. Yet, the imparting of the lesson was of significant importance to Shadrack, who three years before had dreamed about her visit in his dream of the window, river, and voices, doubtlessly those of Sula's and Nel's, outside his cabin door.

Chapter Four
Liminality and the Search for Self in *Song of Solomon*

The ultimate quest for self and its realization is found in Morrison's third, award-winning novel, *Song of Solomon* (1977). It tells the story of the quest for cultural identity by its hero, Macon (Milkman) Dead III. Like Pecola's and Sula's, Milkman's story focuses on his turbulent rite of passage into adulthood, into manhood. But more important, like Shadrack's, his journey also reveals the significance of the historical and cultural self. Milkman cannot become complete until he (re)connects the loose historical cords of his memory. He must "re-remember" them.

Consequently, here, too, setting—community and neighborhood, Detroit, Danville, and Shalimar—remains of paramount importance. For it is through the now-familiar kaleidoscopic view of communal black life, which we have come to expect from Morrison, that we find the dramatization of the conflicts her protagonist(s) must experience, confront, overcome, or resolve in the process of becoming. *Song of Solomon* is closer to Ralph Ellison's *Invisible Man,* however, than to her earlier works; it, too, combines the epic quest with the *bildungsroman* motif and the search for the Grail of identity theme.

Like *The Bluest Eye* and *Sula,* as a novel of formation, *Song of Solomon* ultimately aims to achieve a total, authentic personality for its hero. Here, too, secondary characters serve as mentors who aid the protagonist, as educators, companions, and lovers. Pilate, Guitar, Hagar, Ruth, and Macon Sr. mediate, interpret, or reflect the alternatives available to Milkman. As in the other texts, however, *Song of Solomon* loudly echoes Morrison's contention that authentic existence emerges from self-affirmation, from making choices that lead to self-ownership, rather than from a life of being-for-others. The ultimate choices are Milkman's to make, much as they are Pecola's, Sula's, and Shadrack's.

Here, again, we find that the central tension of the text emerges from the significant roles the protagonist must assume in charting the direction of a life that must skirt "bad faith and falsehood" and be steeped in the existential responsibility to act, to "express an effort of the will or a freedom of the will."[1] Milkman's ultimate task is to achieve "a strong and centered sense of self, a self that accepts responsibility for his past and reaches out in love for others."[2] As Morrison told Mel Watkins, "If there is any consistent theme in my fiction, I guess that is it—how and why we learn to live this life intensely and well."[3]

Morrison makes this explicit through the lessons Milkman learns directly and indirectly from his family, the Deads, whose very name signifies forfeited beings, empty lives: inauthentic existence. Thus, we must begin with an examination of the experience that each member brings to Milkman, the initiate, to assess the lessons he must learn, accept, or reject.

Inauthentic Experience—Ruth Foster Dead

The most significant experience of inauthenticity is offered by Milkman's mother, Ruth Foster Dead, who by herself "ain't nobody" (67).[4] Reared after her mother's death by an affectionate and elitist father, Ruth grows into womanhood without a personal identity, as the extension of her father, the only black doctor in the community. She is known by most as "Dr. Foster's daughter," as the only offspring of the most important black in town. A young lady of manners and culture, Ruth enjoyed an elegant childhood, nurtured by the warmth of her father's love and the sanctuary of his twelve-room citadel. Located on "Not Doctor Street" (named after her father), it offered the trappings of black middle-class life, all hidden behind its heavy doors.

At sixteen, Ruth marries Macon Dead II, a "colored man of property" (23), who by the age of twenty-five would inherit the doctor's place as the most prominent black in the community. He moves into the doctor's mansion: although rather fond of his daughter, the doctor had grown tired of her "steady beam of love" (23) and is relieved when Macon joins them. After two children and fifteen years in a loveless marriage, Ruth gives birth to Milkman, their only son. Made to face daily a husband whose jealousy and hatred keeps her "awkward with fear" (10), Ruth lives in the memory of the near-incestuous relationship she shared with her now-deceased father. We are told that "she had never dropped those expressions of affection that had been so loveable in childhood" (23). Macon's contempt for Ruth had begun when he found her in bed with her father's dead, bloated body, kissing his fingers.

Ruth verbalizes her awareness of her lack of personal identity when she describes herself to Milkman:

I was pressed small. I lived in a great big house that pressed me into a small package. I had no friends, only schoolmates who wanted to touch my dress and my white silk stockings. But I didn't think I'd ever need a friend because I had him [her father]. I was small, but he was big. The only person who ever really cared whether I lived or died . . . he cared . . . and there was, and is no one else in the world ever did. (124)

To ensure her father's continued presence, validate her identity, and find meaning while locked in a sterile marriage, Ruth visits her father's grave at night. There she renews that "cared-for-feeling" (124) she had received from him during his lifetime.

The poignancy of Ruth's sitting—empty, alone, and lonely—talking to her father's grave verifies, once again, Morrison's effort to demonstrate the consequences of inauthentic existence characterized by a life that is falsely and selfishly lived for "the Other." Unlike Sula, who guarded her "Me-ness" and unlike Eva, who built her own home (that is, life) according to her own specifications and design, Ruth chooses to accept her father's home, and it "pressed [her] into a small package" (123).

That she is a "small woman" results directly from her personal action, for at no point does she rebel, as does Nel, for example, or her daughter First Corinthians. Other significant influences come into play, however, paramount among which is Ruth's not having had the advantage of a mother to nurture her through significant stages of her girlhood and young womanhood, as did Sula and Nel, whose mothers, despite their life-styles and personalities, were there for their daughters. Ruth's marriage by age sixteen suggests her problem. The fundamental bond between mother and daughter that Morrison in her work insists is necessary is lacking here. She has not had the luxury of blossoming with her mother's milk; her growth is thus artificial, like Pecola's, who is forced to drink white milk from a cup. Although she receives love from her father, Ruth appears psychologically damaged and incomplete. She confuses her father's love, much as Pecola confuses Cholly's, and mistakes it for possession, perhaps out of fear that her father, like her mother, might neglect or abandon her.

Morrison's naming of this character is thus not coincidental. All three names—Ruth, Foster, and Dead—suggest dependence and absence. Like her biblical counterpart, Ruth is devoted and loyal to the

point of forfeiting all rights to her personal life. In her relationship
with the doctor, we hear resonances of the Old Testament Ruth who
tells her mother-in-law, Naomi, "Entreat me not to leave thee, or to
return from following after thee for whither thou goest, I will go; and
where thou lodgest, I will lodge; . . . Where thou dies, I will die, and
there I will be buried: the Lord do so to me, and more also if out but
death part thee and me" (Ruth 2: 16–17).

Not even in death does Ruth Foster Dead's fear of or loyalty to her
father abate. She confesses, "It is important for me to be in his presence, among his things, the things he used, had touched. Later it was
just important for me to know that he was in the world" (124). In life,
she is "fostered" or nurtured by this relationship, and it robs her of a
self that results in meaningful, personal development. In short, it
leaves her "dead" though alive.

The water mark she observes on her fine mahogany table, which like
the vessel that made the mark is imported and forced into the house,
symbolizes her flawed existence, which is also externally anchored:
"Ruth looked to the water mark several times during the day. She knew
it was there, would always be there, but she needed to confirm its
presence . . . she regarded it as mooring, a checkpoint, some stable
visual object that assured her that the world was still there; that this
was life and not a dream. That she was alive somewhere, inside, which
she acknowledged to be true only because a thing she knew intimately
was out there, outside herself" (11). Like the table, Ruth's life is
blemished and unwhole.

It is also her propensity to fashion an identity outside herself that
leads her to validate her essence and being through Milkman, whom
she sees as her one aggressive act. He is, after all, the living evidence of
the last time her husband made love to her. Here, as with her father, an
unwillingness to let go marks the relationship; she nurses her son far
beyond infancy for her own satisfaction: "He was too young to be
dazzled by her nipples, but he was old enough to be bored by the flat
taste of mother's milk" (13). He gains the name "Milkman" at age six
when Ruth's ritual is discovered by the town's gossip.

There is little doubt that Ruth's indulgences provide her with the
physical contact her husband denies her, but her motives are not merely
the fulfillment of sexual needs. This act may even represent efforts to
compensate for the aborted relationship Ruth experienced from her
mother's death, which would have fractured the nurturing process.
Morrison maintains that one person cannot raise a child: "Two people

should or either a whole community. And a community is not simply made up of women. It is made up with men in it and the men are as important as the women . . . they are different. They do different things."[5]

Significantly, Ruth's nursing of Milkman also simultaneously meets her maternal need to nurse and nurture. We can, in fact, say that in *Song of Solomon* Morrison looks more expansively at her treatment and characterization of the female character through the complex theme of motherhood, of woman-as-mother, by exploring further the roles of woman-as-(wet)nurse and woman-as-nurturer.

Clearly, the implication here is that woman is more than maker of children, a label that could easily be appended to such Morrison mothers as Pauline, Geraldine, and Hannah, who seem to have no time—no quality time—for their children aside from obligatory care. Ruth is their polar opposite. She lives for her children, especially Milkman, and gains complete personal satisfaction from them, in spite of the fact that Milkman later perceives her as perverted and sullying.

Morrison broadens as well her treatment of the mother/son relationship explored in *Sula,* with some significant differences. Whereas Eva destroys Plum to give him new life, Ruth provides her son with nourishment to sustain his life, making it possible for him to become physically a man while symbolically remaining a child. Aware of this, Milkman objects: "I know I'm the youngest one in this family, but I ain't no baby. You treat me like I was a baby" (50). Morrison explains, Ruth "played house with her son—taking him into the little room and nursing him as though he were a doll, a toy."[6] Ruth did not want her son to mature into adulthood, hence the symbolic overextension of his childhood and the significance of his name, Milkman.

In the end, both Eva and Ruth offer Morrisonian variations of the classical and mythological earth mother, for both are creative, life-giving forces and devouring ones as well. Both women sacrifice themselves for their children; but Eva, unlike Ruth, sacrifices her son as well. Ultimately, Eva's willingness to do so makes her more authentic than Ruth, who remains fostered in a world of Deads. Ruth's failure to explore her own interest leaves her not only in a very circumscribed life, but those she chooses to defer her life for do not reciprocate. In fact, they return her love with distaste. Macon hates her. Milkman, who once defended her against his father, comes to see her as "silly, selfish, queer, and faintly obscene" (123). Her father, we are led to believe, had eventually chosen death over her love.

Rejected by father, husband, and son, Ruth remains inauthentic, empty, and isolated, because she has no independent self on which to stand. Paradoxically, she does not go insane like Pecola or die like Sula. In fact, we are told that "she was fierce in the presence of death, heroic even, as she was at no other time. Its threat gave her direction, clarity, audacity" (310). What is the source of this undaunting strength? It is certainly not hate, as in Eva's case. No doubt, her sense of motherhood and the complexity of her role in this regard have something to do with this tenacity. Nevertheless, in his quest for authentic existence Milkman concludes that without a personal identity, his mother had very little to give.

Inauthentic Experience—Macon Dead II

As a successful realtor, Macon Sr. has much to offer his son. Unfortunately, what Macon absorbed is mostly material; Macon believes that "Money is freedom . . . the only real freedom there is" (163). Like Ruth's life, Macon's is fundamentally inauthentic; he is monomaniacally driven to acquire material wealth, at all costs, personal and human. Cold, objective, and calculating, he is said to be a "difficult man to approach, a hard man, with a manner so cool it discouraged casual or spontaneous conversation" (15).

Ample evidence is offered to support this description. When Mrs. Baines, a tenant in one of his slums, informs him that she is unable to pay the rent ($4) because she has to feed her children, he replies, "Can they make it in the street, Mrs. Baines? That's where they gonna be if you don't figure out some way to get me my money" (21). When loneliness drives Porter, another tenant, to threaten suicide, Macon surfaces at the site, not to save a life, but to collect his rent. "Put [the gun] down and throw me my goddam money!" he hollers. "Float those dollars down here, nigger, then blow yourself up" (25).

The source of this insensitivity and callousness lies in Macon's past. Like Ruth, Macon blossomed during an early childhood that was quite ideal. He, too, was nurtured by a father who loved him; and he, too, had a mother who died when he was young. The love he received was not fashioned solely in a world of materialism and conspicuous consumption, however, as in the case of Ruth. We are told that Macon worked side by side with his father on their farm at Lincoln's Heaven from the age of four. As the name of the farm suggests, it represented the freedom that his father, a former slave, had hoped to gain and enjoy as a landowner.

Moreover, it suggests that theirs was a long-range enterprise, since it would take sixteen years before a profit would be realized.

The Deads, Macon Sr., his son, Macon II, and his daughter, Pilate, were landowners. In fact, Macon Sr. was killed while protecting his land in a dispute over a question of ownership. One might safely conclude, however, that the material value of the land was unbeknownst to Macon Sr., much less to the twelve-year-old Macon II at the time of his father's brutal murder. In fact, the murder provided the youth with a significant moment of truth. He apparently learned that land had a financial value as well as a spiritual, natural value. This event was also to be the source of Macon's own harshness and brutality in the future.

Despite the absence of economic profits, it is apparent that Macon II had benefited from the profits of "economy," in the Thoreauvian sense, offered by Lincoln's Heaven. He had harvested a higher and more ethereal life from both his salient relationship with his father and from the oneness his father apparently shared with the soil, with an organic and natural world. As the farm's name suggests, theirs was a Walden Pond–like existence, an Edenic world whose fertile soil enhanced bonding between father and son as well as providing the fulfilling experience, that of seeing the products of their joint labor and of being at one with the earth.

The Emersonian and Thoreauvian lessons of nature—physical and spiritual, related to the cultivation of the land and, by extension, to the oneness between tiller and soil—were the immediate legacies and profits of the maturing, growing manchild. Macon's reminiscence of his childhood residence reverberates with the sounds and sights of Thoreau's Walden Pond. "It was a little bit of a place. But it looked big to me then . . . About eighty [acres] of it was woods. Must have been a fortune in oak and pine; . . . We had a pond that was four acres. And a stream that's full of fish . . . And we had fruit trees. Apple, cherry" (51). In his recollection one hears strains of Emerson's discourse in the essay "Nature": "Almost I fear to think how glad I [was]. In the woods too a man cast off his years . . . and at what period soever of life is always a child." It is a reminiscence that brings joy to Macon's life; he "paused and let the smile come on" (51). The commodity he recalls is not only the material but the process and result of nature's ministry. It is not merely economic profit but the joy the land and his father's philosophy of the economy of a simple life that bring Macon a brief moment of happiness and wholeness.

Macon was robbed of his material birthright as rightful heir to
Lincoln's Heaven, however, when his father was brutally killed, the
land illegally taken, and he, along with Pilate, expelled. Aware of no
original sin to justify the expulsion, Macon aborts the teachings of his
father's examples, replacing them with a life of bitterness, alienation,
and quiet desperation, "laying up treasures," as Thoreau writes in
Walden, "which moth and rust will corrupt and thieves break through
and steal." Assessing his struggle in a Marxist dialectic of "haves"
versus "have nots," he is driven, like a machine, to own things, as he
becomes a member of the bourgeoisie. He marries Ruth strictly for
personal advancement rather than for love. She is no more than another
piece of real estate to which he holds the keys.

His tunnel vision is thus not unlike Pecola's obsession with blue
eyes. His reaction to his negative experience is not unlike her response
to Yacabowski. Although he had been shown, through his apprenticeship with his father, a meaningful approach to a more ethereal life, he
aborts it for one that, though materialistically fulfilling, requires the
prostitution of his spirit. Much as Pecola subordinates her creative
anger in place of shame, Macon "subdued his self, his magic, and
became an acquirer of things and subordinated everybody to it."[7] A
slave driver to himself and others, Macon is not able to overcome his
obsession with material treasures, even during old age, and consequently cannot live simply and wisely. He remains locked in an acrid
life of unfullfilment that manifests itself in the hatred, criticism, and
disapproval of his family, particularly his wife: "His hatred for [Ruth]
glittered and sparkled in every word he spoke to her" (15).

Much like Ruth, Macon is driven by emptiness to seek vicarious
meaning through Milkman. Hardened by the betrayal of his early childhood experiences, he tells Milkman: "Own things. And let the things
you own own other things. Then you'll own yourself and other people
too" (55). Ironically, he fails to see that he does not own himself, for he
has become enslaved to the things he owns. The slum houses, Packard,
and position do not fulfill him: "he felt as though the houses were in
league with one another to make him feel like the outsider, propertyless,
landless wanderer" (27). Spiritually impoverished and physically alienated from self, family, and community, Macon wanders in the dark one
evening to his sister Pilate's house, where, unnoticed, he listens outside
her window to her singing: "Near the window, hidden by the dark, he
felt the irritability of the day drain from him" (29–30).

Aware of Macon's sense of nothingness and his inability to love others or himself, Milkman rejects his father. In fact, Milkman does everything he can to be different: "Macon was clean-shaven; Milkman was desperate for a mustache. Macon wore bow ties; Milkman wore four-in-hands. Macon didn't part his hair; Milkman had a part shaved into his. Macon hated tobacco; Milkman tried to put a cigarette in his mouth every fifteen minutes. Macon hoarded his money; Milkman gave his away" (62–63).

Milkman lacks interest in the choices made available to him by his parent and by his community: "All he knew in the world about the world was what other people had told him. He felt like a garbage pail for the actions and hatred of other people. He himself did nothing" (120).

Aunt Pilate

Pilate, Milkman's aunt, provides him with the ultimate example of authentic existence. From birth, her life has been a continuum of self-actualization. Although her mother died before giving birth to Pilate, the baby "inched its way headfirst out . . . dragging her own cord and her own afterbirth behind her" (28). Signifying a propensity toward self-determination, Pilate is without a navel, a phenomenon that makes her, like Sula, a pariah. More important, it symbolizes her independent and untrammeled spirit; she is not anchored to anyone or anything.

Accepting early her enigmatic characteristics, Pilate makes living itself an art. She becomes both the creator and creation of her art. At twelve she appended her name to her person in a snuffbox that hung from her ear. When the discovery of her smooth stomach thwarts her early efforts to acclimate to the environments in which she found herself, even in her domestic relationships, she "threw away every assumption she had learned and began at zero. First off, she cut her hair. That was one thing she didn't want to have to think about anymore. Then she tackled the problem of trying to decide how she wanted to live and what was valuable to her. When am I happy and when am I sad and what is the difference. What do I need to know to stay alive? What is true in the world?" (149) Like Eva who designed her own Alhambra to self, Pilate lays the foundation of hers by starting at the bottom, "zero."

In contrast to her brother, Macon Sr., and his wife, Ruth, who are driven by external motivations and materialism, Pilate lives a life epitomizing ethereality. Unlike Macon, she remains committed to the higher laws, a spiritual life, that she discovered as a child on Lincoln's Heaven, loving what Thoreau calls "the wild not less than the good." Her life continues the Walden Pond experience she had known at Lincoln's Heaven, physically and spiritually, for she lives in a cabin, a narrow, single-story house on the periphery of town, where she is not a mere traveler in nature but a harvester of its true offerings and strange liberty. Furnitureless and devoid of such modern conveniences as gas, electricity, and running water, Pilate's home provides an avenue through which to live deliberately. It stands in contrast to her brother's citadel, whose emptiness makes it "more prison than palace" (9) and drives him to seek sanctuary outside Pilate's window, where he listens to her improvised song and witnesses her spontaneous life, one firmly grounded in her organic relationship with nature: "No meal was ever planned or balanced or served. Nor was there any gathering at the table. Pilate might bake hot bread and each one of them would eat it with butter whenever she felt like it. Or there might be grapes, left over from the winemaking, or peaches for days on end . . . If another got a half bushel of tomatoes or a dozen ears of corn, they ate them until they were gone too" (29). It is the "economy" of life rather than the economics of life that interests Pilate.

To Milkman, this woman with "berry black lips" "looked like a tall black tree" (37–38). The sun and odor of pine and fermenting wine permeate the curtainless home of this once "wood-wild girl," who made it a habit to chew on pine needles. Pilate is literally the daughter of Nature: motherless, she was nurtured by the forest during her childhood. Macon tells us that she even smells like a forest. Thus, like Eva, Pilate is a prototype of the "Great Mother," "Mother Earth." As William K. Freiert explains, Pilate's "smooth stomach was a sign that she was not born from human woman—in mystical terms, she is Earth, the Mother of all."[8]

Unlike in *Sula*, however, the concern is not with this archetype's capacity to love or propensity to destroy. Milkman has no need to question Pilate, as Hannah does Eva, about her ability to love. Although she, too, like Macon II, witnessed the senseless killing of her father, and was robbed of her material legacy, Pilate does not relinquish the salient values, relative to caring, that her father sought to teach her by admonishing her not to "leave a body behind" (148). Consequently, her life's agenda is not engulfed, like Macon's, in desperation, bitterness, and hate. She is able to show compassion and love, even for her brother who though once a compassionate sibling now hates her. A spiritual healer, Pilate, we are told, "had a deep concern for and about human relationships" (150).

It is in the significance of these qualities that her name lies. In his blind ritual of naming, Pilate's father thumbed inadvertently through the Bible, choosing "a group of letters that seemed to him strong and handsome" (18) to name his mysterious self-birthing girlchild. He saw in them "a large figure that looked like a tree hanging in some princely but protective way over a row of smaller trees" (18). Although discouraged from naming his child after the killer of Christ, her father was adamant. He explained that he had mediumistically foreseen an individual whose sensitivity and strength would lead her to tower above others. Pilate fulfills her father's prophecy: "A tree grounded in her own principles, she thus protectively towers over those about her, not only by her six-foot height but by the ascendancy of her love."[9] Here, again, we see another instance of Morrison's more positive use of biblical referents. As may be further seen in her use of themes, scenes, and names that she takes from biblical mythology, especially in *Song of Solomon,* Morrison's use, as Anne Mickelson notes, is "extensive and varied." It enriches the text rather than suggests, as Edelberg would have us believe, that Morrison wishes to imply that the Bible is "the wrong book for blacks."[10]

Having eked out her own truths about life, Pilate can guide Milkman on his path toward self-realization. By carrying a geography book to denote where she has been and by collecting rocks from each place to denote her determination, her role is specifically that of spiritual guide, the polar opposite of his parents. Barbara Christian correctly notes that central to the novel is the conflict between the values of Pilate and her brother, which Milkman has to resolve for himself.[11] After helping to bring Milkman into the world, she was prepared to direct him away from his fruitless (Dead) existence. She "has as much to do with his future as she had with his past" (35).

Milkman's Quest

By age thirty, Milkman has a need to escape the existential vacuum of his pointless and aimless life, as well as the effort of those around him to work "out some scheme of their own on him . . . Everything they did seemed to be about him, yet nothing he wanted was part of it" (165–66). As the self he discovered in personal reflection suggested, he "lacked coherence, a coming together of the features into a total self"

(69–70). Milkman resolves to take control of his life by declaring, "I want to live my own life" (223), a pronouncement that, like Nel's self-affirming, "I am me," achieves *nommo,* creating or self-creative.

Yet, it must be noted that his pronouncement does not imply a desire for the experimental life that remained salient to Sula but for a transcendental life, one that surpasses the material world of his parents. Initially, in fact, Milkman identifies material wealth, gold nuggets, as the source of the independence and authenticity that he desires. This is not surprising given his father's orientation and the apparent impact he has had on his son. Believing that the "treasure" Pilate keeps hoisted in a green sack in the ceiling of her home is the gold cache she had taken from him, Macon sends Milkman to steal it. Considering his promised share a means of beating "a path away from his parents' past" (180–181), Milkman agrees, enlisting the assistance of his "main man," Guitar. When the would-be-gold turned out to be a bag of bones, Macon sends Milkman to Danville, Pennsylvania (his father's home), where he believes the gold must still be buried. Failing to find it there, Milkman goes to Shalimar, Virginia (his grandfather's home), in an effort to retrace Pilate's journey and discover the hidden gold.

Paradoxically, although he goes in search of his father's material legacy, Milkman discovers instead his personal treasured legacy: his genealogy, cultural identity, and historical community, embedded in the folklore of his parent's communal past. Ironically, then, in his effort to "beat a path from his parents' past," he literally stumbles right into it. Thus, Milkman, as Susan L. Blake notes, "progresses from his father's values to Pilate's. He sets out seeking gold, his father's concern, but ends up seeking family, Pilate's concern."[12]

His journey to self, in fact, had begun at age twelve—a significant age of initiation—when, despite his father's forbidding, he visited and met his Aunt Pilate. Her role as guide and educator—as *pilot,* as her name suggests—is that of *griot:* She is guardian of cultural and familial lore. This is made evident from the outset, for she provides Milkman with a sense of self in history. Pilate is the first person to tell him about his grandfather and Lincoln's Heaven. Significantly, this begins the process of his reclamation of name, of his identity. Armed with the information Pilate has given him, Milkman is able to get his father to add to the lore about his grandfather, Macon Dead I, who had been given the name "Dead" by a drunken soldier. "[H]e asked him who his father was. Papa said, 'He's dead.' . . . in the space for his name the fool wrote, 'Dead' comma 'Macon' " (53). Illiterate, the grandfather remained unaware of the fostered identity but agreed to keep it later on when his wife, a free Indian, explained that the new name would wipe out his past of slavery. Ironically, by accepting the surname "Dead," he erased more than the slavery experience—he obliterated his entire legacy, a goldmine that included a past rich in culture, history, and community, that extended beyond slavery to a rich African past. His action thus robbed his progeny of their legacy, relegating them to a life of materialism and inauthentic existence.

Milkman's journey to Danville and Shalimar places him in the presence of his past. It marks the point of his separation from the false community of the Deads and begins the rite of passage that will result in his incorporation into his ancestral community, allowing him to transcend his present fostered existence in a spiritual flight to self. At this point his status as liminal hero is most evident.

According to Arnold Van Gennep, in any given society, an individual's life is characterized by a succession of stages. At each stage, or passage, the individual must undergo a tripartite journey involving a *rite de separate* (separation), a *rite de marge* (transition), and a *rite d'agregation* (incorporation). The three phases in combination constitute rites of passage. The *rite de marge,* sometimes referred to as the *liminal* phase (from the Latin *limen,* or margin), represents a period when he is "betwixt and between."[12] No longer assigned to a culturally defined social position or status, the initiand finds himself in limbo.

According to symbolic anthropologist Victor Turner, for the initiand, the liminal state represents, in a sense, a period of "structural impoverishment." He is an individual who is both "no longer classified" and "not yet classified."[14] The final objective is incorporation: the movement of the individual from one well-defined position to another. He is separated for all time from one status and reintegrated into the society in a new status.

Although Milkman's journey indeed imbues him with the characteristics of the hero of tradition, making him akin, for example, to Ulysses, Oedipus, and Daedalus,[15] his journey must also be understood within the context of traditional African culture. Here, ritual incorporation generally occurs after the initiand has been carefully tutored in the art of communal living. In this traditional world, which embraces the living and the "living dead," the significance of the collective society takes precedence over the individual. "Consequently, initiation rites . . . not only introduce the novice to adult life, but more important, they educate him, providing instructions in traditions, institutions, and, above all, in the revered ethical values of the group."[16] Turner correctly notes that the liminal phase is a period not only of structural impoverishment but also symbolic enrichment.[17]

Wearing the trappings of his middle-class identity—a three-piece suit, light blue buttondown shirt, Florsheim shoes, and a watch— Milkman arrives in Danville fifty-eight years after his father left. While there, he is treated benignly by Reverend Cooper and Circe who, as *griots* recite his family history, helping him to unravel his muddled past. Like her mythical namesake, Circe (who saved Macon's life after his father's death) points Milkman in the direction of Hunter's cave, where, she tells him, he will find his grandfather's remains, for he had not been properly buried. To find the cave, which with the passing of time had become hidden in the woods, Milkman climbs a hill and twenty feet of deep rock, after crossing a creek that runs in front of the cave. With the exception of a collection of boards, leaves, rocks, and a teacup. he finds "nothing at all" (252) in the cave.

Milkman's Danville experience marks the point of his separation from the Deads and begins a rite of passage that will allow him to metaphorically take flight into self. His ascension to the cave as initiand (his cultural womb) is an act that brings him closer to aggregation—to his grandfather and lost community. It necessarily involves the symbolic testing of strength and ritual cleansing (water is the element used here), which he experiences in the climb and by his submersion in the creek, that the liminal hero must encounter. Significantly, this is a process that requires him to shed his artificial past, symbolized by his soiled, torn clothing and his shoe, which he removed, indicating his humility as initiand. This ritual cleansing is a form of new birth. Upon reaching the creek's edge, for example, he breathlessly hoists himself from its body, much in the manner that Pilate birthed herself after her mother died during delivery. Most important, this action signifies his completion of the preliminary preparation of his flight to self.

Rebirth is also experienced in Shalimar, when initiatory priests and elders, Luther and Calvin—names one readily associates with reform and rebirth—take him on a hunt. In the woods he overcomes fear by defeating Guitar's challenges to take his life, and he indicates his preparedness for manhood by firing the rifle at the hunted bobcat. In town, the elders end his educational initiation when they ritualistically share the catch with him and give him the bobcat's heart. His middle-class status was of no use to him here:

There was nothing here to help him—not his money, his car, his father's reputation, his suit, or shoes . . . all he had started out with on his journey was gone: his suitcase with the Scotch, the shirts, and the space for bags of gold; his snap-brim hat, his tie, his shirt, his three-piece suit, his socks, and his shoes. His watch and his two hundred dollars would be of no help out here, where all a man had was what he was born with, or had learned to use (280).

The striking parallel between Milkman and the recurring image of the peacock in the text clearly indicates this metamorphosis. Royster correctly notes that "the peacock is a symbol of an unregenerated Milkman."[18] When he goes with Guitar to rob Pilate, Milkman sees a white peacock whose inability to fly peaks his interest. Guitar explains that the peacock cannot fly because he has "Too much tail. All that jewelry weighs it down. Like vanity. Can't nobody fly with all that shit." Guitar advises: "Wanna fly, you got to give up the shit that weighs you down" (179–80). A significant part of the waste that inhibits Milkman's flight to a more "centered sense of self" is his false identity, for in spite of his name, he is not without history and community; in short he is not "Dead." To take flight he must somehow abort this baggage.

Milkman's experiences in the Blue Ridge Mountains and Shalimar allow him to finally divest his fostered self, the life that has become a burden; like the peacock's vanity, it had weighed him down. Like an African initiate who enters the forest at puberty, symbolically dies through the act of circumcision, and returns to his village a man, Milkman enters the woods of his parents' youth and there, stripped of his social trappings, completes his rite of passage. He leaves the forest a new man, one who has been shaped not solely by the environment but also his distinct choices and actions: by his decision to live, to walk the earth as "Self."

In coming to grips with his whole self, Milkman learns that he cannot circumvent his racial and cultural identity. He can now interpret and understand the sacra and lore that he discovered concisely encoded in Shalimar's folklore about Solomon, the flying African. He is in fact the spiritual and biological heir of Solomon, who rebelled against his bondage in slavery with his flight back to Africa and whose history is recorded in Pilate's blues song about "Sugarman," which he heard for the first time when he visited her home at twelve and now hears in Shalimar's children's ring game:

Jake the only son of Solomon
Come booba yalle, come booba tambee
Whirled about and touched the sun
Come konka yalle, come konka tambee

Left that baby in a white man's house
Come booba yalle, come booba tambee
Heddy took him to a red man's house
Come konka yalle, come konka tambee

Black lady fell down on the ground
Come booba yalle, come booba tambee
Threw her body all around
Come konka yalle, come konka tambee

Solomon and Ryna Belali Shalut
Yaruba Medina Muhammet too.
Nestor Kalina Saraka Cake.
Twenty-one children, the last one Jake!

O Solomon don't leave me here
Cotton balls to choke me
O Solomon don't leave me here
Buckra's arms to yoke me

Solomon done fly, Solomon done gone
Solomon cut cross the sky, Solomon gone home.
(306–7)

In unraveling the deeper meaning of the children's game Milkman comes to know his paternal roots. He learns that his paternal grandfather, Jake, was reared by Heddy, an Indian, who had rescued him when his father's effort to carry him to Africa failed. His great-grandmother, Ryena, had lost her mind as a result of the desertion. Jake would later marry Singing Bird, the daughter of his surrogate mother, and they bore two children, Pilate and Macon II. As Susan Willis notes, "The end point of Milkman's journey is the starting point of his race's history in this country: slavery. The confrontation with the reality of slavery, coming at the end of Milkman's penetration into historical process, is liberational because slavery is not portrayed as the origin of history and culture."[19]

Milkman finally discovers his inheritance and whole self at the end of his journey when he concludes that the bones in Pilate's "treasure" are Jake's remains. Milkman and Pilate return to Shalimar and give the remains an appropriate burial shortly before Pilate is killed by Guitar. Milkman comes to understand why Pilate's name was appended to her ears. He concludes: "When you know your name, you should hang on to it" (333). Knowing his identity leads to full integration of his self. At the end of the novel he takes flight to signify his ultimate actualization and freedom. He is, without a doubt, the true heir of Solomon.

The Meaning of Flight

Through the tale of Solomon, the flying African, and its central metaphor—flight—Morrison returns to the central issue of existential freedom: the ultimate responsibility of the individual to chart the direction of, to pilot his or her life. Everything about Pilate's life indicates that she has understood and assumed this responsibility. Milkman realizes this at the moment of her death. He concludes: "Without ever leaving the ground, she could fly" (304). But this, too, he concludes, was true of Solomon: "For now he knew what Shalimar knew: If you surrendered to the air, you'd ride it" (341).

Morrison thus suggests here again, as she has done through Claudia and Freida, as well as Shadrack and Sula, that self-actualization and personal freedom are achieved through individual actions. Without a doubt, the central trope flight "is associated with a spiritual triumph."[20] But as Susan Blake notes, there is a contradiction here. "Although Milkman cannot achieve identity without recognizing community, the identity he achieves is individual."[21] The same would be true of Solomon, whose solo flight—which theoretically reunited him with one community—required that he abort wife and family, at least in Morrison's lore. Blake calls attention to the paradox: "On the one hand, his quest leads Milkman to his kin, close and remote; on the other hand, it sets him apart, like the quest hero of myth and fairy tale . . . On the one hand Solomon is clearly Milkman's hero and model . . . On the other, he dramatically violated the principle of responsibility to other people that Milkman has to learn in order to discover him."[22] As she indicated to Ntozake Shange, however, Morrison is quite aware of this inherent contradiction. If flight is a trope for achieved selfhood in *Song of Solomon*, it is not unproblematic. Flight, Morrison conceded, "also has that other meaning in it; the abandonment of other people." Flight is paradoxically "triumph and risk"—

tragedy and triumph. In the end what seems to matter to Morrison is not the violation ("you do leave other people behind"),[23] but the willingness to become exceptional, to take the leap. Morrison will save the question of limitation, as we will see, for *Beloved*.

New Depth in Black Male Characters

With her treatment of Milkman as the protagonist, Morrison offers a more in-depth treatment of the black male character than, with the exception of Shadrack, has been heretofore witnessed in her work. Through her characterization of Milkman, we are given a better rounded view of and careful insights into the complexity of the black male, his aspirations, frustrations, and determination. Morrison confessed that her effort here was intentional; she wanted to look at the world from a man's point of view: "I've never considered looking at the world and looking at women through the eyes of men [before]. It fascinated me. It really was, for me, the most incredible thing in the world. I was obsessed by it . . . I mean trying to feel things that are of no interest to me but I think are of interest to men, like winning, like kicking somebody, like running toward a confrontation; that level of excitement when they are in danger."[24] Morrison accomplishes much of this task through the salient friendship and camaraderie that Milkman and Guitar share, but also through the other men. Here, unlike in *Sula*, for example, the men are not superficial or immature; Porter, Macon, Milkman, and Guitar are in fact most complex.

In Porter's story, for example, we see that men, too, can be desperately alone and lonely. That he has a need for more than physical love is suggested in the subtle allusions that make him a Christ figure. He is laden, like Jesus, with a love for humanity, hence the significance of the name "Porter." "I love ya all . . . I'd die for ya, kill for ya. I'm saying I love ya . . . Oh God have mercy" (26), he tells a crowd that mocks him much as Christ was mocked while on the cross. He acknowledges the congruence of their experiences when he states: "You [Jesus] know all about it. Ain't it heavy?" (26). The implications are related not solely to the difficulty involved in loving one's fellowman but also to doing so unselfishly, without the expectation of reciprocity. This quality is lacking in black male/female relationships, Morrison seems to have concluded in her previous assessments. Porter's unselfish love is responsible, in the end, for Corinthian's resurrection from the "Dead," from the meaningless world of materialism of her father's home.

Morrison's treatment and characterization of Macon Sr. is equally significant. Although we may not approve of his actions, we are given ample information to understand the source of his behavior. This does not lead to justification but to empathy. We feel the depth of Macon's loneliness and emptiness, for example, in the poignant image of this ostensibly powerful man hiding in the dark outside Pilate's house. For a brief moment we are drawn into the chaos within him. More important, Macon does not abandon his family, as Boy-Boy does. Although we may conclude that he perceives them as his possession, we must acknowledge that the territorial instinct is also present. He seems willing to guard and protect that which is his, in spite of his inability to openly show affection.

The intricacy of Morrison's black male characters is seen, however, in the special friendship that develops between Guitar and Milkman. It is akin to that which developed between Nel and Sula, in that there seems to be reciprocity until, through misunderstanding, one experiences betrayal. These men also differ from Nel and Sula in that they are independent of each other, each complete within himself. Nevertheless, like Pilate, to whom he introduces Milkman, Guitar serves as mentor; he is a friend "wise and kind and fearless" (47). Above all, Guitar seems to be a surrogate father, replacing Macon, whom Guitar does not resemble in any way. Milkman considers Guitar "the only sane and constant person" (106) in his life. He finds sanctuary in Guitar's home as well as a willing listener and an understanding friend in his more experienced comrade. Guitar shows sensitivity to Milkman's confusion when he tells him, "Looks like everybody's going in the wrong direction but you, don't it?" (106), at the point that Milkman was thinking about his inability to conform. He encourages Milkman to assume the responsibility for his own life. "You got a life? Live it!" he tells him (184).

In spite of his admirable qualities, however, Guitar is potentially dangerous, as his membership in the Seven Days, a vigilante group, suggests. He lacks not only Pilate's shamanistic powers but, more important, her spirit of forgiveness and love for humanity. Like Macon II, he harbors and is enslaved by a deep hatred of whites as a result of his father's brutal death at the hands of whites. The degree to which this hatred becomes a destructive force for Guitar is manifested when he joins the Seven Days. Insecure and paranoid, he is unable to trust anyone, even his devoted friend. When Macon evicts Guitar for back rent, he holds Milkman responsible and considers it a breach of their friendship. Desperate for money, he agrees to accompany Milkman on his search for the lost gold, but believing that Milkman is "not being serious" (104), he is not trusting. He tells Milkman, "I'm nervous. Real Nervous" (227). Convinced that he has been betrayed by Milk-man, whom he believes does not intend to uphold the agreement to share the buried gold, Guitar stalks him to kill him. Paradoxically, he reveals his intention to kill Milkman. When Milkman asks why he has chosen to tell him, Guitar responds, "You're my friend. It's the least I could do for a friend" (301).

Guitar seems honest in his response: He is torn between commit-ment to his friendship and his membership in the Seven Days, his only apparent source of a sense of place. Ironically, in counseling Milkman, Guitar has told him that everyone has desired his life. Now, it becomes obvious that *everyone* is indeed all inclusive, for it includes his best friend. In the end, Milkman makes the ultimate sacrifice and gives his life to his friend: "You want my life?" he asks Guitar, "You need it? Here" (301). Consequently, even here there is a paradox, for in the final moment between the two, Milkman experiences triumph when he learns the ultimate sacrifice: "Not love, but a willingness to love" (226), by unselfishly giving oneself to mankind, by meeting the chal-lenge of his friend-become-nemesis, Guitar.

Male/Female Relationships

Through Milkman's relationship with Hagar, his cousin, Morrison continues to illustrate the detrimental effects of male/female relation-ships that result when in romantic love one willingly forfeits self for the love of "the Other." Ironically, Hagar's demise does not result from the incestuousness of the relationship or her abandonment by Milkman after he grows tired of her dependence. Initially, Milkman was the aggressor and Hagar the reluctant prize. By the third year of their relationship, however, she has made Milkman's life more important than her own. She tells Ruth that Milkman is "my home in this world" (138). She commits, in the world of Morrison's fiction, a cardinal sin. Although the relationship lasts an unusually long time, by the twelfth year, Milkman has grown bored with her accessibility: "Her eccentrici-ties were no longer provocative and the stupefying ease with which he had gotten and stayed between her legs had changed from the great good fortune he'd considered it, to annoyance at her refusal to make him hustle for it, work for it, do something difficult for it. He didn't even have to pay for it. It was so free, so abundant, it had lost its fervor. There was no excitement, no galloping blood in his neck or his heart at the thought of her" (91).

Morrison next uses one of the most powerful "masculine" tropes of her canon to convey the negative place Hagar, having become a "permanent fixture in his life" (97), came to occupy in Milkman's world: "She was the third beer. Not the first one, which the throat receives with almost tearful gratitude; nor the second, that confirms and extends the pleasure of the first. But the third, the one you drink because it's there, because it can't hurt, and because what difference does it make" (91). Like Sula, who had confused love with possession, Hagar wants to own Milkman, even if she has to kill him. Psychologically distraught, she is unable to wield a fatal blow symbolic of castration (she uses such phallic symbols as a knife and ice pick) when, after stalking him for months, she finally catches him. Undoubtedly, she would have killed a part of herself had she succeeded.

In words that seem to capture the crux of Morrison's argument, throughout her collected works, relative to "doormat women" Guitar tells Hagar:

You think because he doesn't love you that you are worthless. You think because he doesn't want you anymore that he is right—that his judgment and opinion of you are correct. If he throws you out, then you are garbage. You think he belongs to you because you want to belong to him. Hagar, don't. It's a bad word, 'belong.' Especially when you put it with somebody you love. Love shouldn't be like that . . . You can't own a human being. You can't lose what you don't own. (309–10)

Finally, Guitar reminds Hagar that if her life "means so little to [her] that [she] can just give it away, hand it to [Milkman], then why should it mean any more to him? He can't value you more than you value yourself" (310). Hagar's death is inevitable; she dies at the moment Milkman stands at the threshold of his manhood.

Communities of Women

This novel, like the others, has several communities of women. Significantly, though composed of threes as before, the clusters are no longer generic, as they are in *The Bluest Eye*. They are eclectic, and the women tend to be more eccentric. For example, Ruth and her daugh-

ters, First Corinthians and Magdalene called Lena, are quite like the
women of Helene Wright's house in that they conform to social conven-
tions. That they spend their time making artificial flowers clearly
suggests the stagnant quality of their false, hollow, virginal lives,
which, paradoxically, also have some stability. These women are not
abandoned to care for themselves by the likes of a Boy-Boy or Jude
Green. Corinthians' educational pursuits and her brief employment as a
maid indicate her desire for personal freedom. When Corinthians falls
in love with Porter, however, she deviates completely from the mold
and role of caretaker and centerpiece for her father's status.

Confessing that she had initiated the task of artificial flower making
in the family because it kept her "quiet," Lena finally gets the strength
to confront Milkman, whom she felt had exploited his role as male heir.
She tells him, "Our girlhood was spent like a found nickel on you"
(216). Like her plant on which he urinated, she withers and dies in the
gloomy world of the doctor's house. Unlike Corinthians who abandons
everything, Lena finds escape in alcohol. Unfortunately, Lena, like the
mother she felt a need to protect always, never gets around to acting, to
doing "something terrible" (215), although she seems to resolve to do
so when she warns Milkman: "I don't make roses anymore, and you
have pissed your last in this house" (218).

A similar complexity can be found among the other significant
cluster of women: Pilate, her daughter, Reba, and her granddaughter,
Hagar, who to some degree are reminiscent of the women in Eva Peace's
house. Their wine making and improvised music illustrate their generally creative and fulfilling lives. Yet, we know from a close examination
of their characters that this remains true of Pilate alone. Although they
are not degraded in their home like Lena and Corinthians, Hagar and
Reba do not seem to benefit directly from Pilate's example of self-
actualization.

They remain confused about love, for example, associating it with
possession and gift giving. They never arrive at Pilate's level of independence or her realization that true love is unselfish, caring, and above all
free. Reba, who gives "away everything she had" (94), is turned "on for
everything in pants" (76), so much such that she is taken advantage of
by men. Hagar is the weakest of the two, however, because she is not
"strong enough, like Pilate, nor simple enough, like Reba, to make up
her life as they had" (311).

Like Eva, Pilate and Reba are deeply engrossed in their role as
mothers. This is particularly true of their instinct to secure and protect

their offspring. When one of Reba's lovers hits her, Pilate comes armed to her defense. She tells him, "Women are foolish . . . and mamas are the most foolish of all . . . Mamas get hurt and nervous when somebody don't like they children" (94).

Unlike Eva, whose behavior suggests that motherhood and love involve the realization of the appropriate time to let go of one's siblings, Pilate and Reba remain devoted mothers, catering to the every desire of their daughters. We get the impression that Pilate wishes to compensate for the years when, abandoned by husband and friends who feared the implications of the absence of her navel, she wandered aimlessly about and Reba did not have a stable home. Hagar, however, is the very reason for settling down. Pilate decides that Hagar "needed family, people, a life very different from what she and Reba could offer" (151). They spend their lives giving Hagar everything she wants, as Reba tells her: "We get you anything you want, baby. Anything" (48). Their propensity to overindulge Hagar begins when she is two and ends with her death. To some degree, then, they are responsible for Hagar's inability to accept Milkman's rejection. She was not accustomed to being told no. As if to justify their behavior, Pilate declares at Hagar's funeral: "And she was *loved!*" (323).

We may conclude in the end that such untrammeled maternal love is as destructive as Macon's blind materialism. Ironically, one may also conclude that the significant difference between Pilate and her daughter and granddaughter lies in the tangible relationships they have established with men. Though the community of women is important, so is the absence of men in their lives. Morrison reminds us that Pilate spent twelve important years of her life in a meaningful relationship with her brother and father, which made her fierce and loving: "Her daughter had less, that daughter's daughter had none. So her relationship to men was curious and destructive, possessive . . . the stuff that Pilate has is not transmitted by DNA; you need other people."[25] There must be a shared responsibility, Morrison maintains, for the child to begin to approach wholeness.

Myth and Mysticism in *Song of Solomon*

Structurally and thematically, *Song of Solomon* draws heavily not only from the world of folklore but also from the worlds of mysticism and magic. Far more than in *The Bluest Eye* and *Sula,* Morrison muddles the division between the real and the fantastic, among folklore, myth, and history. The mythic structure of *Song of Solomon,* as Chiara Spallino notes, is that of the hero's quest myth. It fits well, as noted above, into a pattern of the heroic myth. In fact, it is possible to agree with Leslie Harris that the myth structure is responsible for the cohesiveness of the novel; it prevents it from being meandering and confused.[26] Significantly, however, as Spallino points out, "Morrison's characters . . . are portrayed as mirroring their communities and culture, and it is the strength of the continuity of the Black heritage as a whole which is at stake and being tested here."[27]

Consequently, Milkman's quest, as noted earlier, must also be assessed within the context of an African communal rite of passage. Although allusions to classic myths are visible from the very beginning, as in the Icarusian flight of the insurance agent Robert Smith, Morrison is obviously borrowing from the black "folk stuff" that she knows intimately, including the tale of the flying African. As she reports, "I've heard all my life that Black people could fly, just as I heard the tooth fairy story, and I accepted it. Then I used to read about it in the slave narratives."[28]

Then there is otherworldly Pilate, whose distinct characteristic is the absence of her navel. This, more than the fact that she was apprenticed to a root worker, is believed to endow her with magical powers. As shaman, she is able to assist Ruth in getting Macon to make love to her. Pilate put a small doll on Macon's chair in his office; "A male doll with a small painted chicken bone stuck between its leg and a round red circle painted on its belly" (132). Thus, much like Isis, the wife of Osiris, who is often associated with the dead, Ruth (who is married to a Dead) is able to conceive magically after sleeping with the dead/Dead.

Equally significant is the presence of the mythological shaman/witch Circe in the form of her Morrisonian counterpart. Much in the manner that Circe provides the information that guides Odysseus through the River of Ocean, offering him advice on how to deal with the ghost of Tireseas, Morrison's Circe, with her toothless mouth but mellifluent voice, directs Milkman on his Odysseyan path to self, "Go north until you come to a stile. It's falling down, but you'll see it's a stile. Right in there the woods are open. Walk a little way in and you'll come to a creek. Cross it. There'll be some more woods, but ahead you'll see a short range of hills. The cave is right on the face of those hills. You can't miss it" (247–48). Circe also becomes "healer and deliverer" who guides Milkman to the site of his ancestral past by telling him about his grandmother, Sing. She above all sets him on the correct path to his desired treasure.

It is Pilate, however, who maintains direct contact with her mythic past. She communicates with her dead father, and although unaware of it, she keeps his remains hanging from the ceiling in her home. Morrison thus successfully weaves into her tale here again African cosmological views of the reciprocity that exists between world of the living and the living dead. Simultaneously, she includes folk notions of propitiation, of appeasement, evident in the fact that Macon Dead, Sr. had not been appropriately buried. Circe tells Milkman, "The dead don't like it if they're not buried. They don't like it at all" (247). His ghost returns as an apparition, though not as a poltergeist, until he has been appropriately buried.

Moreover, Pilate is the paradigmatic folk heroine, the trickster as hero. We see her protean quality when she changes both voice and size in going to rescue Milkman from jail. While in the jail, she appears shorter and whines as she speaks. On her way home, however, "Pilate was tall again. The top of her head, wrapped in a silk rag, almost touched the roof of the car . . . and her own voice was back" (209). Milkman's father tells him that, like a snake, Pilate has the power to step out of her skin, and neighbors maintain that she "can set a bush afire from fifty yards, and turn a man into a ripe rutabaga—all on account of the fact that she had no navel" (94).

What seems to remain most important, however, is Pilate's role as *griot:* she knows and guards the family history; her blues song about Sugarman is not a lamentation but a celebration of Solomon, the ancestor who escaped slavery by taking flight. She alone can carry her identity firmly sealed in her person because she alone knows who the family really is, and she alone can pass it on to Milkman to allow him to become fully realized. It is only by tracing his ancestry through the myth to the flying African that he, too, can take flight at the end in a symbolic death that leads to rebirth and transcendence. Interestingly enough, when they meet for the first time, Pilate offers Milkman an egg, a symbol and foreshadowing of the rebirth he will eventually realize. The incorporation of myth and mysticism into the text is inevitable, because they are legacies of the Afro-American experience that is Milkman's.

Through the major characters of *Song of Solomon,* Morrison reveals that the struggle for self is indeed complex. The quest for authentic self inevitably involves the quest for truth, love, survival, and even power

and forgiveness. For most of the characters, the search for external
fulfillment proves unrewarding. Macon is materially rich, but he remains empty. Yet, whether externally or internally, the characters are
marked with a sense of incompleteness that drives them toward some
form of wholeness. Morrison also suggests through her characters that
to achieve some equilibrium, love is paramount—love of oneself and of
one's fellowman.

In the end, Milkman is a riddle solver, as Dorothy Lee points out:
he brings "his treasure . . . the gift of [self-] knowledge . . . to his
people."[29] Only when self-knowledge and self-love are in place can
one experience true transcendence, can one ride the air, "fly" like
Pilate and Milkman, can one sing her/his "song of songs"—her/his
song of Solomon.

Chapter Five
Folklore as Matrix for Cultural Affirmation in *Tar Baby*

Through Jadine Childs and William Green (Son), the pivotal characters in *Tar Baby* (1981), Morrison develops the recurring theme of the quest for wholeness, which we must now deem the sine qua non of her canon. The novel, her fourth, opens with Son, a fugitive who jumps ship in the Caribbean and lands on the Isle des Chevaliers. He hides in *L'Arbe de la Croix,* the luxurious home of Margaret and Valerian Street, white American retirees from Philadelphia. When discovered by Margaret, Son is invited by her husband to join the Street household for the Christmas holidays, much to the displeasure of Margaret, the trusted live-in servants, Ondine and Sydney, and their niece, Jadine, who is visiting from Paris.

At first, Son is looked upon with suspicion, especially by Jadine, who is simultaneously repelled and attracted by him; he is her polar opposite, educationally, socially, and culturally. Ultimately, after she succumbs to his advances, they fall in love and flee to New York in hope of finding a conducive atmosphere for their lives and careers. After traveling to Eloe, however, Son's pastoral hometown in northern Florida, Jadine concludes that the relationship will inevitably fall short of her expectations. According to James Coleman, the New York love affair is an ideal one set apart from outside pressures; it provides a respite before Jadine and Son must test their harmony and newfound wholeness against outside reality.[1] Jadine flies back to New York, then retreats to the islands before returning to her Parisian lover in Europe who had asked her to marry him. In pursuit of the relationship, Son follows Jadine to the island but is diverted when led on a different path toward self-hood and wholeness by island resident Mary Therese.

Like Milkman, Sula, and Pecola, Jadine is lost in a state of liminality. She is trapped between two cultures: black and white, European and African-American. Orphaned at age twelve, she was reared by Ondine and Sydney in Philadelphia. When they left with

Valerian for the Isle de Chevalier, she was sent to Europe to complete her formal education. A graduate with a degree in art history from the Sorbonne and a successful model, recognized internationally for her beauty, Jadine lives in the fast lane and is primarily interested in "making it"—in material success.

Jadine

Given her Europeanization, Jadine, unlike Shadrack and Milkman, is completely oblivious to race and, specifically, to her African-American roots. So divorced is she from black culture, from that which is her legacy as a black American, she thinks of it in strictly stereotypical ways. Her contemplation of her engagement to a Frenchman evidences her confusion about questions of race: "I wonder if the person he wants to marry is me or a black girl? And if it isn't me he wants, but any black girl who looks like me, talks and acts like me, what will happen when he finds out that I hate ear hoops, that I don't have to straighten my hair, that Mingus puts me to sleep, that sometimes I want to get out of my skin and be only the person inside-not American-not Black-just me?" (48)[2] Jadine's problems are not related to gender; she sees herself strictly in terms of class, as an independent, successful professional.

Jadine is made to confront her cultural heritage, however, when challenged haphazardly in Paris by an African woman who wears her heritage with pride and dignity:

The vision itself was a woman much too tall. Under her long canary yellow dress Jadine knew there was too much hip, too much bust . . . so why was she and everybody else in the store transfixed? The height? The skin like tar against the canary yellow dress? The woman walked down the aisle as though her many colored sandals were pressing gold tracks on the floor . . . Her hair was wrapped in a gélee as yellow as her dress. The people in the aisles watched her without embarrassment, with full glances instead of sly ones. (45)

Disgusted at the sight of Jadine, a black woman who has obviously forgotten her roots, the African, "with the confidence of transcendent beauty" (48), once outside insultingly spat at her.

Like Pecola, Jadine is made to evaluate herself on the basis of a visual exchange that offers an external definition of self by the "Other." She, too, is affected by the damaging "look." She reacts at first with indifference, but she is unable to transcend the implications of the "woman's insulting gesture," which in the end has successfully "derailed her" and "shaken her out of proportion" (47). Unlike Pecola, however, Jadine is not riddled with shame and self-hatred; thus, she is not destroyed by the African woman's look. It becomes an important catalyst, nevertheless, for "the woman had made her feel lonely in a way. Lonely and inauthentic" (48).

Barbara Christian correctly notes, "Morrison uses the image of the African woman in the yellow dress as a symbol for the authenticity that the jaded Jadine lacks. It is this woman's inner strength, beauty, and pride, manifested in the defiant stance of her body, that haunts Jadine's dreams and throws her into such a state of confusion . . ."[3] Jadine is made aware of what Therese would later inform Son is Jadine's loss of her "ancient properties," which Angelita Reyes defines as "those sacred and psyche-cultural bonds of the Past."[4]

Although she flees her Parisian lover and retreats to her island home in the Caribbean, Jadine does not find sanctuary there. The island does not provide immediate resolution. In fact, Jadine is made to confront head-on her effort to escape her black culture when she recalls with Valerian a conversation she had with his son, Michael. Having left Morgan Street of her childhood days in Baltimore, she explains, she had grown to appreciate "Ave Maria" rather than gospel music and was convinced that "Picasso is better than an Itumba Mask" (74). She has lost any sense of a "communal landscape."[5] Unlike the black sealskin coat that she puts on to adorn herself, black culture had little value for Jadine, and she readily shed any residue of it.

Jadine's interactions with Son cause her hidden contradictions to surface. In their first serious exchange, she reveals an inability to think of blacks in less than stereotypical terms. The encounter is significant because it reveals the confusion that forms the crux of her personal conflict, although she thinks she is offering support for her independence.

Upon first seeing Son, Jadine immediately suspects that he has "rape, theft, or murder on his mind" (91). When she tells him about her initial reaction, she acknowledges not knowing what he had wanted to steal "from us" (118). When Son questions her failure to distinguish herself from the Streets, Jadine explains further, "I belong to me. But I live here" (118). Significantly, her response discloses the dichotomous quality of her life: On the one hand achieving cultural independence seems important to her; she must not "belong" to anyone but herself. On the other hand, by living in the Streets' household she has inevitably grounded herself in their culture. She is rooted in cultural confusion. When the exchange between Jadine and Son intensifies to confrontational levels, Jadine reveals how deeply ingrained her stereotypical views of blacks are. She exclaims, "You rape me and they'll feed you to the alligators. Count on it, nigger. You good as dead right now" (121). His response, also based on a stereotype, elicits a revealing reaction:

"Rape? Why you little white girls always think somebody's trying to rape you?"
"White?" She was startled out of fury. "I'm not . . . you know I'm not white!"
"No? Then why don't you settle down and stop acting like it" (121).

To Son, in behavior, convictions, and actions, Jadine had come to typify her adopted culture. Defensively, Jadine rushes to deny what her external behavior had suggested. During the exchange, she maintains that she, in fact, could not be defined externally by being told "what a black woman is or ought to be" (121). Rather than attempting to escape part of her identity, she argued, she had merely sought to define herself with the criteria she had identified as important.

During an ensuing physical exchange between the two, reminiscent of the ritual dance of the sexual behavior of street dogs on the prowl, Son attempts to explore Jadine's libido through scent. Although she can "smell" Son, Jadine comes to the realization that his body odor, which she associates with his blackness, is not as offensive as she had imagined it to be; she is, in fact, attracted by it: "He had jangled something in her that was so repulsive, so awful, and he had managed to make her feel that the thing that repelled her was not in him, but in her. That is why she was ashamed. He was the one who smelled. Rife, ripe. But she was the one he wanted to smell" (123). Initially, what Jadine finds offensive is Son's raw blackness, symbolized by his Rastafarian dreadlocks, which he wears with defiance and pride to affirm the African heritage within which he is firmly rooted: "His hair looked overpowering—physically overpowering, like bundles of long whips or lashes that could grab her and beat her to jelly. And would. Wild, aggressive, vicious hair that needed to be put in jail. Uncivilized, reform-school hair. Mau Mau, Attica, chain-gang hair" (113). Paradoxically, what she "smells" in him and knows exists in her is their black heritage, which he wears with dignity and she tries to deny with her noncommittal definition of self. But as Reyes notes, it is not only Son that Jadine fears. "She also fears intimacy with her heritage."[6]

Thus, Jadine's status as orphan is significant, for it may be ascribed to her in diverse ways. At the crucial age of twelve, a point of transition from childhood to adolescence, she is deprived of parents to nurture and guide her. There is no Pilate in her life. Unlike Pilate, who passes the legacy of her cultural heritage to her nephew, Milkman, Ondine does not perform this function for Jadine. As Coleman states, Ondine's "commitment to Jadine, while well-intentioned, has been lacking. Ondine has not provided the example of folk caring and loving that she talks about in her conversation with Jadine."[7] Moreover, Ondine and Sydney's marriage is a significantly barren one. Their sterility extends beyond the biological to the cultural, for as "Philadelphia Negroes" they seem far more interested in the welfare and care of white culture than in their own lives. Ondine tells Jadine, "I know my kitchens. Better than I know my face" (39), suggesting the degree to which her familiarity with the lives of her white employers supersedes her familiarity with herself.

It is significant that the Streets were totally responsible for Jadine's formal education. As patrons, they paid for her travels, lodging, clothes, and schools. It is also significant that she, unlike her relatives, is not a domestic. Although she ostensibly gives Margaret secretarial assistance, she dines with the Streets and is waited upon by her aunt and uncle in the same manner that they wait upon their employers. Jadine is thus a complete product of their program and culture.

Paradoxically, by entrusting Jadine's development to the Streets, Sydney and Ondine orphan their niece further; in effect, they put her outdoors in the streets, to borrow from the narrator's distinction in *The Bluest Eyes* between being *put out* and being *put outdoors*. Neither Margaret nor Valerian has been a model parent to their only child, who has been abused by his mother. By educating Jadine in Europe, the Streets crystalize her status as orphan; the foreign culture makes an impact on the young child at her most transitional and impressionable years. If Jadine behaves like a white girl, as Son suggests, then it is because she has been nurtured on white culture and weaned away from her black heritage. As she does with Pecola, however, Morrison holds Jadine partially responsible for her life in the discourse of the text.

Ultimately, Jadine desires to escape the cultural maze that has bound her. She seeks independence and self-definition, yet she seems to be irrevocably locked into a life defined by others, whether Son, Ondine,

the Streets, or the Parisian lover to whom she returns at the end. In the
final analysis, she desires to "feel herself," to journey forward on her
own impetus, like the star Son asks her to imagine herself to be. "Don't
try to see it. Try to be it" (214), he tells her. But to do so, she would
inevitably become alone, like the solitary star in the dark sky.

Son

In contrast to Jadine, Son admits to feeling "out of place" (160) in
the Street's home, signifying his lack of attraction to Western culture,
within which he remains in solitude, a drifter without an anchor:

Propertyless, homeless, sought for but not after. There were no grades given in
his school, so how could he know when he had passed? He used to want to go
down in blue water, down, down, then to rise and burst from the waves to see
before him a single hard surface, a heavy thing, but intricate. He would
enclose it, conquer it, for he knew his power then. And it was perhaps because
the world knew it too that it did not consider him able. The conflict between
knowing his power and the world's opinion of it secluded him, made him
unilateral . . . he never wanted to live in the world their way. (166)

Son had sufficient nourishment from his community in Eloe, Florida,
however, a place where there were no white people but where fraternity
with Blacks, "the last thing left to him" (133), could be found.
   Less interested in materialism than Jadine, Son lives a more leisurely
life, desiring only his "original dime" (170), the sheer pleasure that one
gets from working. He refuses "to be made" by Jadine who, afraid that
he will be "a yardman all [his] life" (265), insists that he become both
employed and degreed. When she specifically insists that he pursue a
law degree, he responds, "I don't want to know their [whites'] laws; I
want to know mine" (263). This pronouncement makes him akin to
Sula, Nel, and Milkman, whose desire to be independent and self-
reliant provided impetus in their lives at one point or another. More
important, it suggests that his interest is more in the "economy" of life
than in the economics, which is validated by his more ethereal life. His
laws are the "higher laws" of nature, the spiritual rather than the
material.
   What Jadine wants for Son is a similar experience to hers in terms of
a professionally trained career, one that would result in economic success. Son vows, however, that he will never succumb to her plans for his

career, because they would lead to class genocide as far as he is concerned. Son asks, "You think I won't do all that company shit because I don't know how? I can do anything! Anything! But I'll be goddamn if I'll do that!" (270).

That the fundamental difference is rooted in cultural perception is suggested by the narrator, who explains, "He wanted to do things in time—she wanted them done on time" (266). The significant difference between a diachronic and synchronic perception of time—linear versus cyclical—suggested here is accepted as an essential difference in African and Western cultures.[8] Jadine, saturated with (jaded by) Western culture, maintains a more linear perspective, while Son, the progeny of African culture, maintains a more cyclical one. It is in this regard that Son's Rastafarianism must be understood. His dreadlocked hair is more than chic; he is Africa's son/Son, the bearer of its culture and values, its black Messiah come to save Jadine from the street/Streets of Babylon.

Morrison does not, however, suggest that their differences are irreconcilable. As James Coleman suggests, although they are quite different, "each has something which is vital to the other."[9] According to the narrator, "Each knew the world as it was meant or ought to be. One had a past, the other a future and each one bore the culture to save the race in his hands. Mama-spoiled black man, will you mature with me? Culture-bearing black woman, whose culture are you bearing"? (269) Resolution is not readily forthcoming, however.

In another instance of the disapproval through which Son reveals his jealousy, because of what he perceives as a conflict between Jadine's loyalty to him and her loyalty to her white educational benefactors, he accuses her of preferring whites to blacks: "You turn little black babies into little white ones; you turn your black brothers into white brothers; you turn your men into white men and when a black woman treats me like what I am, what I really am, you say she's spoiling me" (270). His tirade culminates in the tar baby folktale, which provides the novel with an organizing myth. Son delivers his modified version of the tale: "Once upon a time there was a farmer—a white farmer . . . And he had this bullshit bullshit bullshit farm. And a rabbit. A rabbit came along and ate a couple of his . . . ow . . . cabbages. . . . So he got this great idea about how to get him. How to, trap . . . this rabbit. And you know what he did? He made him a tar baby. He made it, you hear me? He made it!" (270) Identifying with the hero of this folktale, Son sees Jadine as the tar baby that Mr. Street creates and later uses to trap him. But his tale only serves to alienate Jadine, who does not share his perception of the past, which to her is a "medieval slave basket" (271). Aborting the past, she tells him as she prepares to leave, is more productive: "There is nothing any of us can do about the past but make our own lives better, that's all I've been trying to help you do. That is the only revenge, for us to get over. Way over. But no, you want to talk about white babies; you don't know how to forget the past and do better" (234).

After he realizes that he has lost her, Son makes a desperate effort to revive their relationship with intentions now of giving her anything that she wants—that is, conforming to whatever she wants him to be. As Strouse relates in his account of an interview with the author, "high-yellow Jadine, cut off from all the funk and blackness of her past, essentially bought and raised by a white man, cannot be the woman Son needs her to be—she can't live with him in the briar patch; and he cannot live without her. The tar baby and the rabbit lock in a fatal embrace."[10] And so Son is trapped at last, hooked on her, and as the folktale suggests, the more one struggles against entrapment, the more trapped one becomes.

Folklore and Mysticism

Later Morrison weaves into her novel another tale, the story of the Ant Kingdom, which can be seen as an elaboration upon the male/female relationship theme. Its underlying message is that for two basic reasons neither dreaming nor its security are available to women. To begin, she suggests that women are the embodiment of security themselves. Moreover, life places such demands on them that they simply do not have the time for such leisure. The legend of the soldier ants here, most of whom are women, makes this message clear. The nature of the relationship between the male and female ants and between Jadine and Son clearly has a strong parallel.

Therese views Son mythologically, as a descendent of the island's mythical blind horsemen. His mission is to rescue her in the way that these warriors had rescued the island's blacks. " 'I told you!' said Therese. 'He's a horseman come down here to get her' " (107). According to Josie Campbell, Jadine "is able to feel 'unorphaned' when Son tries to reorient her culturally toward the values of her own race."[11] Once she decides that she can no longer accept his values or his world, she leaves him, fleeing back to the embrace of the dominant (white) culture. Like the male ants, Son dies, at least emotionally, because of Jadine's rejection. He is not totally helpless in his fate, however. In fact, he plays a major role in determining it by allowing himself to be taken in by her charm and beauty.

Jadine's response to Son evokes an important part of the tale concerning the queen bee: "This little Amazon trembled in the air waiting for a male to mount her. . . . Frenzied, he flies into the humming cloud to fight gravity and time in order to do, just once, the single thing he was born for. Then he drops dead, having emptied his sperm into his lady-love" (291). Like the "little Amazon," Jadine, too, is "airborne, suspended, open, trusting, frightened, determined, vulnerable—girlish . . ." (291). She does not act independent of him; at first, she is almost submissive, accepting his abuse of her, thereby becoming his true victim.

There is ambivalence here, for we can also argue that Son is reacting to his sense of powerlessness and frustration, which forces him to resort to physical prowess rather than independent action. Perhaps he is reacting, not because of anything Jadine does but out of his own insecurities. Ultimately, however, Jadine reclaims her self-control. She refuses to accept his dictates. Here we witness the power of the word, the voice, creating in this case Jadine's freedom from submissiveness. Jadine says, "I can't let you hurt me again. You stay in that medieval slave basket if you want to. You will stay there by yourself. Don't ask me to do it with you. I won't" (271).

Needless to say, their relationship is doomed, partly because of who Jadine is, out of his class (a product of Valerian Street's creation), but mostly because of Son himself. Son does not share Jadine's white values. She embraces the materialistic society and accepts its standards of living. He, on the other hand, tries to reject the standards of the dominant culture. He even censures Jadine in his tar baby folktale tirade concerning the kind of education she has and wants him to have. Given these conflicts and his own insecurities and unwillingness to believe in and to create a better future for both of them, Son's destiny seems apparent. Given Jadine's insistence upon letting the past remain just history and living for the present and the future, her destiny is also apparent. Morrison herself best evaluates their situations: "Both are inadequate positions today, unless you are very sure. She [Jadine] hasn't enough of what he has and he [Son] doesn't have enough of what she has."[12]

Above all, in *Tar Baby* Morrison utilizes fully folklore and mysticism

that were latent in *The Bluest Eye* and *Sula* and were developed in *Song of
Solomon*. In *Tar Baby,* she affirms what had been heretofore implied in the
text: together mythology and folklore form a matrix for cultural affirmation. As the main characters—Jadine, Son, and Valerian Street—journey
through Morrison's topsy-turvy world, they are exposed to a magical
realm of existence. Whereas the boundaries between myth and reality
were muddled before, in *Tar Baby* they seem to disappear completely.
Here Morrison does more than merely make allusions to myth and
folklore, here the genre provides the novel's title and its central themes.
In addition, she continues to weave into her discourse elements of
mysticism—conjuration, superstitions, and spiritual visitations.
Through out the interaction between the physical and the spiritual
worlds, an element of the African continuum—which has become a
dominant characteristic of her writings—is made evident. Through this
technique, Morrison is able to show how her characters fit into the
scheme of things—historically and perhaps even futuristically—as they
seek self or cultural affirmation.

In their search for self-hood, Morrison's characters come to realize
that there are boundless levels of existence to be experienced in the
physical and spiritual world. In fact, their traditional, limited concepts
of life prove to have little impact upon many of their inexplicable
experiences, such as the unexpected encounters with mysticism. For
example, throughout *Tar Baby* one witnesses the recurrence of the
interrelationship between the living and the living-dead, indeed, an
inversion of them in the cases of Valerian and Jadine. Yet, it is through
Valerian in particular that the element of mysticism is most acutely
developed.

Valerian Street migrated to the Caribbean Islands in search of a more
meaningful, peaceful life. He is periodically visited by his deceased first
wife of ten years in the greenhouse of his Caribbean home. Having
become accustomed to spiritual visitations, he finds the greenhouse—
his separate, private domain—a perfect place for such visits. Valerian
"was not alarmed by her visits; he knew he conjured them up himself,
just as he conjured up old friends and childhood playmates who were
clearer to him now than the last thirty years were, and nicer" (143).

On this mysteriously intriguing island Valerian ultimately comes to
terms with his spirituality, at least to some degree, whereas in the past,
prior to leaving America, his life reflected emptiness and mere material, physical realities. His new sense of reality includes the existence of
the spiritual as well as the physical realm. To be sure, he has a better

understanding of his past acquaintances, now that he is operating on a higher, spiritual plan. Still, it is not until the revelations at the Christmas dinner concerning his wife and her physical abuse of their child that he better understands their personalities and actions. For him now, just as for Pilate in *Song of Solomon*, the mystical world is real and can offer meanings incomprehensible in the tangible world, regardless of racial background. Clearly, then, Morrison suggests that a reconciliation of the spiritual and the physical worlds is necessary if a more complete personality, cognizant of the existence of both, is to emerge. Valerian makes such an attempt in his acknowledgment of the two levels of existence.

Heretofore, Valerian, like Macon Sr., operated on the premise of what society defines as real and meaningful. These things include material wealth, job security, a family, and a home. Ostensibly, he is successful in achieving these ends; a close scrutiny, however, will reveal that he has failed. Although his family's business is successful (its candy factory has even produced a candy bearing his given name), his marriage has been unfulfilling. Retiring from a top position in the family business, he settles in a Caribbean home with his second wife, Margaret (a former Maine beauty queen, twenty years his junior), and his son, Michael. Moreover, the ghost of his first wife has become a frequent part of his household. Her visitations are due in part to his boredom and empty marriage. His present wife had perversely taken out her loneliness and frustrations on their innocent son during his early childhood. Valerian's family and home life are a sham.

After accepting the validity of the spiritual world, Valerian uses his power of conjuration when it is needed; nonetheless, he is totally unprepared for his power to conjure up the spirit of the living. The narrator asserts that "he was astonished to see—unconjured—his only living son in the dining room last night . . . Michael seemed to be smiling at him last night but not the smile of derision he usually had in the flesh; this was a smile of reconciliation. And Valerian believed that was part of the reason he invited the black man to have a seat, the forepresence of Michael in the dining room. His face smiling at him . . . was both the winsome two-year-old under the sink and the thirty-year-old Socialist" (143–44). Valerian has conjured up the spirit of his nonconformist son, who influences his life in a positive way by functioning as his conscience, reminding him that he has not yet paid his dues to the victims. (Michael is the victim of his mother's warped revenge; Son is a victim of society.)

Clearly, the spiritual and the physical worlds complement each other, as together they are able to create a higher level of consciousness and existence for Valerian. Without the intervention of the liberal spirit of his son, Valerian would have probably reacted racially, for example, to Son's intrusion in his home, especially since Son was found hiding in his wife's closet. His wife, Ondine, Sydney, and Jadine initially react to Son in a prejudiced manner. Still, Valerian's behavior is rather inconsistent. He had earlier callously fired his two native servants, Therese and Gideon, without the benefit of a warning, which does nothing to support his evolving enlightened sense of liberalism.

Communities of Women

The theme of the community of women recurs in *Tar Baby*. It surfaces when Jadine and Son visit Eloe, Florida, some time after they had fled the island for New York. Eloe "embodies all the blackness she had long struggled to escape."[13] Here as well Morrison intertwines the worlds of the living and the living-dead. While there, they are to spend their nights at Son's Aunt Rosa's home, since they are not married and are dissuaded from spending them at Son's father's home for moral reasons. While at Aunt Rosa's, Jadine's moral consciousness is kindled when the older woman discovers the younger nude in bed and offers her a nightgown. Jadine accepts, but not without shame and guilt. Later, after Son falls asleep, a community of women of the past and present (representing both the living and the living-dead) of both their lives make a visitation. They crowd the little dark bedroom, protruding their breasts:

Cheyenne got in, and then the rest; Rosa and Therese and Son's dead mother and Sally Sarah Sadie Brown and Ondine and Soldier's wife Ellen and Francine from the mental institution and her own dead mother and even the woman in yellow. All there crowding into the room . . . spoiling her lovemaking, taking away her sex like succubi, but not his. He fell asleep and didn't see the women in the room and she didn't either but they were there crowding each other and watching her. Pushing each other—nudging for space, they poured out of the dark like ants out of a hive. (258)

The mystical intrusion of "the night women" ruins Jadine's vacation, and the thought of them continues to negatively influence her relationship with Son even after they return to New York. According to

Edelberg, the night women are "the keepers of 'sacred properties' "[14] that is, they are one's natural instincts and cultural inclinations. Jadine is jealous of these "mamas who had seduced him" (262) and of their influence on Son. She fears, moreover, their intentions where she is concerned; "the night women were not merely against her (and her alone—not him), not merely looking superior over their sagging breasts and folded stomachs, they seemed somehow in agreement with each other about her, and were all out to get her, tie her, bind her. Grab the person she had worked hard to become and choke it off with their soft loose tits" (262).

Although Jadine does not see it, the night women represent a positive force. Like the communities of women in *The Bluest Eye, Sula,* and *Song of Solomon,* they bind together, bent on destroying that negative, unconscious part of Jadine's identity. As Barbara Christian asserts, Morrison "makes an attempt . . . to figure out the possibilities of healing and community for her women characters."[15] Thus, these women can be said to be interested in healing Jadine of her inauthenticity, trying to restore the ancient properties she has lost as a result of losing touch with her culture. Each of the women represents an authentic existence in that none has lost her contact with her culture. Conscious of their culture, "the night women have condemned her [Jadine] and so has the narrator."[16] The narrator asks, "Culture-bearing black woman, whose culture are you bearing?" (269).

The use of the breast evokes the idea of the mother or nurturer. Morrison demonstrates here "her interest in the nurturing characteristics of the black community."[17] On a broader, symbolic level, the woman is the nurturer of her people, the culture-bearer for her race. The night women simply want to nurse Jadine into a healthy mental attitude toward her culture. Jadine is given two chances to be saved from her own unconsciousness, and in both instances her rescuers are the communities of women. The first one is the African woman in yellow who acts as a community of one, bearing the culture because she knows it.[18] The second one is the culture-bearing breast women.

In both instances, Jadine rejects their services as culture bearers. In the case of the former, Jadine, once her consciousness is challenged, flees from her "adopted" culture (Paris). With regard to the latter, she, challenged while immersed in the black culture in Eloe, later flees back to the "adopted" culture (Paris). Hence her flight reflects a futile cycle. Whether or not she benefits or learns from the messages of the culture bearers, they still exist. As Morrison explains, "They distribute it [the culture] and they remark on it."[19]

No Happy Ending, but Possibilities

In the final analysis, things do not resolve themselves in Jadine's and Son's favor. Jadine goes back to her former lifestyle in Paris and Son is urged back to his roots. Son returns to the Isle des Chevaliers, futilely looking for Jadine, and is advised by Therese to leave Jadine to her inauthentic existence. Therese informs Son that his own people, the blind, black descendants of slaves who were marooned on the island, are awaiting his return. Campbell has the following to say about the similarities between Son's and the blind horsemen's circumstances surrounding their arrival on the island: "These runaway slaves landed on the island the same way Son reaches the Isle des Chevaliers—born by the 'water-ladies.' "[20] The affinity between the two possibly explains the ultimate bonding that takes place in the end. Son does retreat to the horsemen and is thought to have joined them in their never-ending roaming of the forest. He asks, " 'Therese! . . . Are you sure?' . . . If she answered, he could not hear it, and he certainly couldn't see her, so he went. . . . He ran. Lickety-split. Lickety-split. Looking neither to the left nor to the right. Lickety-split. Lickety-split. Lickety-lickety-lickety-split" (306), like the rabbit thrown back into the briar patch (home).

Morrison has used folklore and mysticism throughout this novel as a matrix for articulating the interlocking nature of the past and the present as well as the spiritual and the physical worlds. She has successfully meshed opposites rather than pit them against each other in an effort to communicate the intertwining nature of things in the universe. In merging the legends with modern-day phenomena and the living with the living-dead in articulating the quest for wholeness, Morrison has succeeded in creating yet another work that can be read and reread for insights into human nature in general and into the human condition as it relates to race, class, and gender in particular. Moreover, the denial of the emergence of a total physical and spiritual being becomes a legitimate concern for Morrison, one which both the characters and the readers must resolve. As for Jadine, her inability to resolve the obstacles in her life prevents her from becoming whole; she fails to resolve the cultural conflict and her personal fragmentation. Son, on the other hand, does emerge as one who gets back in touch with himself, his roots. Hence, he comes close to achieving wholeness in the end, in spite of and, more important, because of the fact that he loses his loved one, a contradiction of his cultural life-style. Therefore, in Morrison's *Tar Baby,* there is no happy resolution for the dilemma of these characters. The author does, however, offer boundless possibilities for an ultimate interpretation of American/African-American culture—past, present and future.

Chapter Six

"Ripping the Veil": Meaning through Rememory in *Beloved*

Although it won neither the National Book Award nor the National Book Critics Circle Award for 1987, stirring a degree of controversy among black writers and critics,[1] *Beloved*, Morrison's fifth novel, won the Pulitzer Prize for fiction in that year. Six years in the making, *Beloved* artistically dramatizes a haunting amalgam of the past and present experiences of an escaped female slave, Sethe, tracing the heroine's quest for meaning and wholeness in slavery and in freedom. Ever present as a reminder of the past is Beloved, the ghost spirit of Sethe's slave child, whom Sethe killed by slashing her throat with a handsaw in what she considered a mercy killing. After haunting her mother's home at 124 Bluestone Road for more than eighteen years, the ghost becomes flesh and, in the guise of a twenty-year-old woman-child (the same age Beloved would have been had she lived), walks into Sethe's house, where she becomes the manifestation of her mother's conscience.

In committing her brutal act, Sethe believed she was sparing the child from the "unspeakable" fate to which most female slaves were heiresses, a deplorable fate breeding abundant tragic consequences. Morrison's characters are well aware of the vulnerable position in which the black slave woman has been placed: "That anybody white could take your whole self for anything that came to mind. Not just work, kill or maim you. Dirty you so bad you couldn't like yourself anymore" (251).[2]

Set in the nineteenth century, primarily in the gruesome pre– and post–Civil War era, *Beloved* is developed through a series of flashbacks. The recollections are triggered when Paul D, a fellow slave from the Sweet Home Plantation, walks back into Sethe's life. But they are also mandated by Sethe's "rememory," a memory "loaded with the past" (70). In spite of her effort to beat back the past, she is unable to transcend it: "Some things you forget. Other things you never do" (36).

The Source of the Story

While the text of *Beloved* is a "product of invention," of Morrison's imagination,[3] she readily concedes that the story is based on fact. It grew out of one of her Random House projects, *The Black Book* (1974), a "scrapbook" of three-hundred years of the "folk journey of Black America."[4] Morrison became aware of the story of Margaret Garner while gathering materials for the text. A fugitive from Kentucky, Garner attempted to kill her children rather than have them re-enslaved when they were all captured in Ohio in 1850. She succeeded in killing only one, however, whose throat she slashed.[5] Interestingly, the several examples of the slave's resistance to slavery in *The Black Book*—including several stories of women who killed and beat their overseers—do not include Garner's. Morrison would save it for her fifth novel. Acknowledging that she had indeed conducted research while writing *Beloved,* Morrison told Martha Darling: "I did research about a lot of things in this book in order to narrow it, to make it narrow and deep, but I did not do much research on Margaret Garner other than the obvious stuff, because I wanted to invent her life, which is a way of saying I wanted to be accessible to anything the characters had to say about it. Recording her life as lived would not make me available to anything that might be pertinent."[6]

Above all, *Beloved* is an historical novel, framed in purpose, thematics, and structure after the African-American slave narrative. Like the paradigmatic *The Narrative of Frederick Douglass, An American Slave* (1847) and *Incidents in the Life of a Slave Girl* (1861), this novel offers the personal accounts of "black slaves and ex-slaves of their experiences in slavery and of their efforts to obtain freedom."[7] Although *Beloved* is specifically Sethe's story, it is also the story of all the slaves of the Sweet Home Plantation of Kentucky: Baby Suggs, Paul D Garner, Paul F Garner, Paul A Garner, Halle Suggs, and Sixo. Thus, it is also, like the major works of the slave narrative genre, the composite story of all slaves and their quest for freedom through flight.

Unlike other significant texts that belong to this unique American genre, *Beloved* requires no call for the abolition of slavery. This is because Sethe's story is narrated to a twentieth-century audience. Nevertheless, in the tradition of this art form *Beloved* successfully chronicles incidents in the exslave's mind, providing the reader with insights not only into Sethe's thoughts and actions but also into the structure and workings of the plantocracy that denied her basic human and political rights. Thus, as is true of the more traditional slave narrative, *Beloved* records the cruelty, violence, and degradation—whether the physical floggings or the psychological fragmentation of the black family—that often victimized slaves, irrespective of age or gender.

Beloved also has a structure akin to that of the slave narrative, which, according to Frances Smith Foster, parallels the "Judeo-Christian mythological structure. . . . The action moves from the idyllic life of a Garden of Eden into the wilderness, the struggle for survival, the providential help, and the arrival into the Promised Land. In addition, the plot of the slave narrative incorporated the parallel structure of birth into death and death into birth which also distinguishes the Judeo-Christian myth."[8] In her narrative, Sethe moves from the near-pastoral life she leads as house slave of the Garners who own Sweet Home, as Halle's wife, and as mother of three to become a chattel statistic in the record book of schoolteacher and his nephews, who become managers after Mr. Garner dies. Though pregnant, she is flogged and her milk taken. Injured, distraught, and bewildered to the point of insanity, Sethe takes flight into the wilderness where, assisted by a young white runaway named Amy, she gives birth to her fourth child, Denver, before crossing the Ohio River into Cincinnati, her New Jerusalem. In contrast to the traditional slave narrator, however, Sethe's story does not end here, for her freedom is short-lived; schoolteacher tracks her down with the intention of returning her and the children to slavery, precipitating Sethe's brutal act.

The Motives for the Telling

What concerns Morrison in *Beloved,* however, is not what history has recorded in the slave narratives but what it has omitted. Foster offers insight into the significant dilemma of the slave narrator who, in the effort to harness support for the abolition of slavery, did not wish to offend the audience. This made compromises necessary. According to Foster, "The nature of these compromises determined the form and content of the narratives."[9] Fundamentally, she continues, "the narrator's fidelity to the reality of the American slave experience was at the risk of offending many Americans who, regardless of their humanitarian beliefs, were, after all, members of the society being criticized. Moreover, the narratives ran the risk of alienating segments of people because the accounts of slavery presented an unsavory view of the South in particular and the United States in general."[10] The caution practiced by the slave narrator was inevitable.

Morrison's awareness of this tempered voice resonates in her conviction that "whatever the level or eloquence or the form [of the slave narrative], popular taste discouraged the writers from dwelling too long or too carefully on the more sordid details of their experience." But, she argued, by "taking refuge in the literary convention of the day," the slave narrator would often "pull the narrative up short."[11]

As Morrison would have Sethe reveal, however, there was another reason behind the careful selection of the events that they would record and the "careful rendering of those that they chose to describe": "every mention of [the] past life hurt. Everything in it was painful or lost" (58). Consequently, Sethe and "Baby Suggs had agreed without saying so that [the past] was unspeakable." (58) Although she would often provide Denver, who yearned for a knowledge of her mother's past, with some information, "Sethe gave short replies or rambling incomplete reveries." (58)

For Morrison the cost of this blocking was exorbitant in the long run. Thus, like the slave narrator who called for the abolition of slavery, Morrison's purpose in *Beloved* is corrective. Through her narrator she aims to expose the wrong and rectify the full story. Conceding that "somebody forgot to tell somebody something,"[12] Morrison states, "My job becomes how to rip that veil" behind which the slave narrator was forced to hide. But this resolution necessarily requires that she "depend upon the recollection of others," that she draw upon the "memories within."[13]

For Morrison this is the significant act of "rememory": "a journey to a site to see what remains have been left behind and to reconstruct the world that these remains imply." Ultimately, then, she seeks in *Beloved* to find and expose a truth about "the interior life of people who didn't write it (which doesn't mean that they didn't have it)"; to "fill in the blanks that the slave narrative left"; to "part the veil that was frequently drawn"; and to "implement the stories that [she had] heard."[14]

What Morrison also unearths at the excavation site is the silenced voice of the black slave woman, for more often than not her story had been told by the black male narrator whose focus was primarily upon his own journey to wholeness. Although the women who appear are not mere fixtures, for through them the horrors of slavery are unravelled, what is generally told is his/tory rather than her/story; her dimmed voice left her to live a life of quiet desperation.

For example, Frederick Douglass informs his readers that it was the "horrible exhibition" witnessed by him when his Aunt Hester was violently beaten by her white male owner that made him aware of his own servitude. Although he describes his first such experience as "the blood stained gate, the entrance to hell of slavery through which [he] was about to pass," and although he reports hearing Hester's "heart-rendering shrieks," Hester never speaks. The reader is denied access to her feelings and thoughts.[15]

When the woman's voice is heard, as in the case of Harriet Jacob's in *Incidents in the Life of a Slave Girl,* its author must hide her identity under a pseudonym, Linda Brent: "I had no motive for secrecy on my own account, but I deemed it kind and considerate towards others to pursue this course."[16] Paradoxically, even her assumed name/voice must be authenticated by a white guarantor, L. Maria Child, who apologetically explains, "I am well aware that many will accuse me of indecorum for presenting these pages to the public; for the experiences of this intelligent and much-injured woman belong to a class which some call delicate subjects, and others indelicate."[17]

Morrison's *Beloved* thus provides the avenue for a resurrected female slave narrator's voice. And it is not only Sethe who speaks: it is her mother; Patsy, "the Thirty-mile Woman"; and Sethe's two girl-women, Denver and Beloved. Above all, one hears the haunting voice of Baby Suggs, whose broken hip is the physical legacy of sixty years of bondage and whose final escape into colors is the only peace she had known in slavery or in freedom. Barbara Christian correctly notes that "Afro-American women writers rewrite the established history by embodying their ancestors' memory in fiction, and as well respond to previous Afro-American women's literature. Contemporary Afro-American women's work then is intertextual as well as reiteration of the restriction based on class, race, gender, imposed on their forebears."[18]

It is within the realm of the black women novelists' effort to literally reclaim their history by writing, to borrow from Christian, "from the inside out," that Morrison's treatment of Sethe's quest for wholeness must be first understood. Paradoxically, Sethe initially appears to be without a sense of liminality. This is due primarily to the untraditional behavior of the Garners, who "ran a special kind of slavery" (140) on their Sweet Home Plantation, where there were no "men-bred slaves" (141). Mrs. Garner, who "hummed when she worked" (139), and Mr. Garner, who "acted like the world was a toy he was supposed to have fun with" (139), treated their slaves "like paid labor, listening to what they said, teaching what they wanted known" (140). The Sweet Home men, we are told, are "Men every one" (10).

But Sethe's inability to recall much of her life before age thirteen, the point at which she came to Sweet Home to replace the recently freed Baby Suggs, suggests that her lack of liminality is counterfeit; it is due in part to her successful act of "disremembering," of consciously obliterating her painful past. Most painful had been the denial and then severance of any semblance of a meaningful relationship with her mother, who had been branded and later hanged because of her daily resistance to slavery.

Shackled by the reality of her childhood experience in slavery, Sethe is uncomfortable at first at Sweet Home; she "had to bring a fistful of salsify into Mrs. Garner's kitchen every day just to be able to work in it, feel like some part of it was hers, because she wanted to love the work she did, to take the ugly out of it" (22). Two years later she was married to Halle Suggs, who would father every one of her four children, more the exception than the rule. The depth of Sethe's innocence as a woman-child is indicated by her naive expectation of a wedding ceremony. But her innocence was also fueled by the action of her slave owners, indicated by Mrs. Garner's wedding gift of crystal earrings. She seemed justified in believing that Sweet Home had indeed become a real home.

With the death of Mr. Garner and the coming of his brother, schoolteacher, and his nephews, however, Sethe becomes aware of her own liminality as she is made to realize that Sweet Home is "a wonderful lie" (221). Besides beating the male slaves, schoolteacher deprives them of their guns and is adamant in teaching them that "definitions belonged to the definers-not the defined" (190). A physiognomist and phrenologist, schoolteacher immediately commodifies his brother's human property by treating them as creatures, as "gelded workhorses whose neigh and whinny could not be translated into a language responsible humans spoke" (125). To verify that they needed "care and guidance . . . to keep them from the cannibal life they preferred" (151), schoolteacher kept a record of their behavior, as a measure of his "scientific" experimentation with them. According to Sethe, "Schoolteacher was teaching us things we couldn't learn. I didn't care nothing about the measuring string . . . Schoolteacher'd wrap that string all over my head, 'cross my nose, around my behind. Number my teeth. I thought he was a fool" (191).

Sethe's liminality is intensified with her growing awareness of her personal status as chattel. It begins when she accidentally overhears a

discussion between schoolteacher and his nephews in which he deni-
grates her humanity by telling his nephews to "put her [Sethe's] human
characteristics on the left; her animal ones on the right" (193). Questioning Mrs. Garner, Sethe learns the meaning of the "characteristics";
discussing the matter further with Halle, she discovers that schoolteacher's brutal intentions may well include the eventual selling of their
children when they were old enough. Resolving to escape north to
freedom to circumvent any effort to fragment their family, Sethe and
Halle make plans to take the underground railroad to Ohio, although
their original plan was to purchase their freedom.

Amidst the deterioration of black life on Sweet Home, Sethe succeeds in getting her children on board the northbound caravan. Before
she can join them, however, she becomes the sport of schoolteacher's
assistants, who violate Sethe by stealing the milk she bears because of
her pregnancy with her fourth child. She is brutally beaten for reporting this heinous crime to Mrs. Garner. Pregnant, barefoot, and mutilated, Sethe escapes to Ohio, to her mother-in-law, Baby Suggs, and
her children, including her "crawling—already?" baby girl, Beloved.
Although Sethe does not arrive in Cincinnati with Halle, she arrives
with Denver, her fourth child, who was born en route.

In her narrative of Sethe's liminality and flight to freedom, Morrison
returns to the site of Sethe's rememory to excavate its hidden treasures,
painful though they may be. Successfully ripping the veil to reach the
level that was "loaded with the past," Morrison finds among the ruins
of the slave experience the often forgotten instrumental roles and places
slave women played and occupied. Significantly, her find includes the
seminal role they played, for example, in the historical caravan to
freedom, the underground railroad. By having a woman conductor
convey Sethe's three children north to freedom, Morrison reestablishes
the role of women in this historically significant avenue of escape. That
she is historically accurate is verified by John Hope Franklin, who tells
us that Harriet Tubman was "easily the most outstanding Negro conductor on the Underground Railroad."[19] Morrison's text offers implications that are more far-reaching, however, for they suggest the importance of recognizing not only Harriet Tubman but also the many others
like her.

Equally important is Morrison's characterization of the female fugitive in her treatment of Sethe's liminality. As one critic noted, even
though the ranks of fugitive slaves "were not swelled with women,"[20]

women did indeed use this popular form of resistance to slavery. Morrison's accurate portrayal of the black slave woman's experience in this regard is confirmed by Deborah Gray White, whose general description of the slave woman between the ages of sixteen and thirty-five may be amply applied to Sethe. "A woman of this age was either pregnant, nursing an infant, or had at least one small child to care for . . . it is during these years that many slave women got their best care."[21]

Married by age fourteen, Sethe was pregnant with her fourth child by age nineteen. Although Sweet Home's Garner prided himself on the fact that his male slaves were men, and not "men-bred slaves," Mrs. Garner betrayed the owners' hidden agenda, revealing that the most important purpose of the slave woman was childbearing. When Sethe informs Mrs. Garner that she plans to marry Halle, Mrs. Garner asks, "Are you already expecting?" (26). When Sethe responds in the negative, Mrs. Garner informs her, "Well, you will be. You know that, don't you?" (26) Sethe had in fact been brought to Sweet Home to serve as much as a sexual mate to any one of the Sweet Home men of her choosing as she had been brought to replace Baby Suggs, who was now too old to either work in the field or reproduce.

That schoolteacher values Sethe for her childbearing capabilities, and thus for the capital she represents, is indicated both by his decision to capture her and return her to slavery and by the punishment that he meted out to his nephew, whom he blames for overbeating his prized woman slave, leading her to escape. "Schoolteacher had chastised that nephew, telling him to think—just think—what would his own horse do if you beat it beyond the point of education. Or Chipper, or Samson. Suppose you beat the hounds past that point thataway" (149). Sethe comes to realize that it was her apparent value as "property that reproduced itself without cost" (228) that had allowed her to enjoy the benefit of a pastoral life on Sweet Home.

If the most important factor impairing the mobility of fugitive slave women was their concern with the welfare of their children, as Deborah White suggests, then the reverse is equally significant in their decision to flee: They did so to ensure their children's welfare. This is the impetus for Sethe. Separated for the first time from her children, especially her infant "crawling already? girl," Beloved, Sethe, who according to Paul D was driven by a love that was "too thick" (203), struggles to reach Cincinnati at any cost. Determined to get to her children, even at the expense of leaving her husband behind, she explains:

All I knew was I had to get my milk to my baby girl. Nobody was going to nurse her like me. Nobody was going to get it to her fast enough, or take it away when she had enough and didn't know it. Nobody knew that she couldn't pass air if you held her up on your shoulder, only if she was lying on my knees. Nobody knew that but me and nobody had her milk but me. (16)

With words that echo Eva's ("I stayed alive for you") and Pilate's ("I would have happily died except for my babies"), Sethe reveals what she envisions her role as mother to be in a conversation with Paul D. "I don't care what she [Beloved] is. Grown don't mean nothing to a mother. A child is a child. They get bigger, older, but grown? What's that suppose to mean? In my heart it don't mean a thing" (45). When Paul D tells Sethe that she cannot protect her Beloved indefinitely and asks "What's going to happen when you die?" Sethe responds, "Nothing! I'll protect her while I'm live and I'll protect her when I ain't" (45).

By casting Sethe in the role of nurturer, Morrison returns once again to the now-familiar image of the great mother as embodiment of the feminine principle. Like Eva and Pilate, Sethe is interested in protecting her family, providing sustenance and life. Here, however, we find not merely the focus on mother as nurturer but as (wet) nurse, symbolized by her full breast, which she uses to nurse both Beloved and Denver. "I had milk," she said. "I was pregnant with Denver but I had milk for my baby girl" (16). We are also told that Sethe "had milk enough for all" (100). The Demeter-like image of the nursing figure is not new for Morrison. Ruth Foster Dead polluted this elementary role by nursing Milkman beyond infancy, suggesting that it provided her with sexual gratification, while Jadine rejected the night women's implication that this primary role is one in which she should be interested. Therese, whose role during slavery was that of wet nurse, seems to instinctively revert to it in her desire to act as caretaker to Son.

With Sethe and Beloved, however, Morrison probes deeper into the psychological network and nature of nursing and the mother-infant bond—the social and emotional relationship between mother and infant—that is its inevitable outcome. Morrison suggests that such a bond is fundamental to the psychological development of both mother and child. Exploring this relationship within the context of a particular historical period and social arrangement—slavery—she addresses yet another of her finds at the excavation site of Sethe's memory: the psychological damage of slavery to the mother-child relationship.

Morrison's examination heightens the intensity of the damage done to this almost instinctive relationship because both children, Denver and Beloved, unlike Milkman and Son, are in their infancy, and they are girls; the mother/daughter relationship is of paramount importance to the socialization process. To compound it, Sethe, the mother figure, is a mere girl herself. Unlike Ruth or Therese, Sethe is a woman-child of nineteen. Having herself been robbed of this crucial bond with her own mother, Sethe is intimately familiar with the psychological devastation her baby girls would be subjected to without her milk. Recalling her own childhood, Sethe reveals that she had been nursed by her mother no more than two or three weeks before she was nursed by a surrogate "whose job it was" (60). Consequently, she had lost access to "the same language her ma'am spoke" (62). Sethe seems to realize that the integration of her girls' egos, in fact, depended upon the milk she has for them. Nancy Chodorow describes the effect that the absence of this parental care may have on the development of an individual's sense of self:

The quality of care [offered by the mother] also conditions the growth of the self and the infant's basic emotional self image . . . The absence of overwhelming anxiety and the presence of continuity—of holding, feeding, and a relatively consistent pattern of interaction—enable the infant to develop what Benedek calls "confidene" and Eric Erikson "basic trust," constituting, reflexively, a beginning of self or identity.[22]

Beloved, in her emotional behavior upon entering her mother's home on Bluestone Road a fully grown adult, attests to the damage that occurs when this process is negatively affected. She is both bitter and insecure.

To be sure, Beloved's emotionalism emerges as much from a sense of rejection—from being deprived of a symbiotic unity with her mother—as it does from a sense of spite and retribution for the brutal murder she experienced at her mother's hand. Despite her "miraculous resurrection" (105), which signals a form of rebirth at nineteen or twenty, Beloved's behavior is for the most part that of a child, even of an infant. Initially, she sleeps most of the day, waking to drink water or be fed. Much like the child Sethe had murdered, the adult Beloved had not yet gained control of her motor skills. Like Sethe's "already crawling?" baby girl, the adult Beloved, though slender, "moved like a heavier [woman] . . . holding on to furniture, resting her head in the palms of her hand as though it was too heavy for a neck alone" (56).

More important, she immediately attaches herself parasitically to Sethe to the point of appearing like "a ridiculously dependent child" (57): "Sethe was licked, tasted, eaten by Beloved's eyes. Like a familiar, she hovered, never leaving the room Sethe was in unless required and told to. She rose early in the dark to be there, waiting, in the kitchen when Sethe came down to make fast bread before she left for work. In lamplight, and over the flames of the cooking stove, their two shadows clashed and crossed on the ceiling like black swords" (57). Beloved's dependence is one of the consequences of her fragmented infancy, the result of the traumatic separation that takes place when her mother sends her ahead on the underground railroad and the abrupt one caused by the murder.

At the point of these separations, one might conclude, Beloved had not developed adaptive ego capabilities that would have made her more independent of her mother. She was not quite two. Her sense of self at this stage emerges for the most part through her mother, who continues to serve as an external ego, mediating and providing Beloved's total environment. Chodorow explains that during infancy the child's mother "acts as external ego, provides holding and nourishment, and is in fact not experienced by the infant as a separate person at all."[23]

With the murder, Beloved never has the opportunity to come into her own, to find a central self by moving beyond the stage of her infantile ego, which at the point of her death had already been damaged. Still mired in the world of her primary identification—her mother—Beloved does not differentiate herself from Sethe when she reemerges eighteen years after her death; her world is merged with Sethe's. When Denver asks Beloved "What did you come back for?," she responds: "To see her [Sethe's] face." "She left me alone by myself" (75). For Beloved, to see Sethe's face is, in fact, to see her own face. It is interesting to note that Beloved remains spirit until her mother names her by providing a tombstone for her grave. Figuratively speaking, Sethe finally returns for Beloved and names her, providing form for her heretofore voided ego and hence making possible her reappearance.

It is thus not surprising that when we enter Beloved's thoughts, through Morrison's masterful use of the stream of consciousness, we learn that Beloved does not distinguish herself from her mother: "I am Beloved and she [Sethe] is mine. . . . I am not separate from her there is no place where I stop her face is my own and I want to be there in the place where her face is . . ." (210). She later thinks: "I want to be the two of us I want to join" (213). Finally, this blurred identity is made evident when Beloved concludes: "You are my face; you are me/You are mine" (216).

In spite of the fact that at this point we cannot ignore that Beloved is a ghost, it is equally significant that much like the child who has experienced a discrepancy "in the early phase between needs and (material and psychological) care, including attention and affection,"[24] Beloved behaves like a psychologically scarred child. As Chodorow tells us, such a denial would develop into "an all pervasive sense, sustained by enormous anxiety, that something is not right, is lacking" in the child. Though an adult, Beloved "never got enough of anything: lullabies, new stitches, the bottom of the cake bowl, the top of the milk. If the hen had only two eggs, she got both" (240). Because of Sethe's sense of guilt, Beloved was able to make and have her demands met: "The best chair, the biggest piece, the prettiest plate, the brightest ribbon for her hair . . ." (241). When Sethe finally begins to complain, it is for nought. "Beloved accused her of leaving her behind. Of not being nice to her, not smiling at her. She said they were the same, had the same face, how could she have left her?" (241).

In treating the theme of the great mother, as nurturant and nursing figure, whose primary responsibility is that of caring for her children, Morrison returns to the concomitant image of the archetypal "terrible mother" as well; for Sethe, like Eva who murders Plum, is a mother who kills her child in order to save its life, or give it new life. Sethe's original intention was to kill all four of her children, not just one. Upon seeing the slave catchers and schoolteacher's hat, Sethe automatically knew that returning to slavery was not an alternative: Her children, now free, would not become slaves again. "I couldn't let all that [the brief freedom they had known] go back, and I couldn't let her [Beloved] nor any of 'em live under schoolteacher" (163). Death, she was convinced, would provide a life that was better than anything she had known or experienced at Sweet Home.

Like the behavior of nesting birds, Sethe's action seems almost instinctive. She could think only of protecting and getting her babies to safety: "And if she thought anything, it was No. No. Nono. Nonono. Simple. She just flew. Collected every bit of life she had made, all the parts of her that were precious and fine and beautiful, and carried, pushed, dragged them through the veil, out, away, over there where no one could hurt them. Over there. Outside this place, where they would be safe" (163). Like Eva, Sethe suggests that time could not be wasted when immediate actions were required.

Morrison's reference to "the veil" here recalls this central and significant trope of W. E. B. DuBois's *The Souls of Black Folk*, specifically his
use of it in "On the Passing of the First Born." Though saddened by the
death of his first child, a son, DuBois celebrates the dead infant's
triumph over the "Land of the Color Line," from whence came "the
shadow of the Veil"—segregation, which he had escaped through
death.[25] Thus, Sethe, like DuBois, sees death as a sanctuary from an
oppressive life. It is important to note, however, that what was true of
Eva is equally true of Sethe: the act of murder was not perceived as a
senseless crime but as a necessity. Hence the significance of Sethe's
action runs much deeper than it appears on surface.

On the one hand, Sethe's goal is to prevent her children from bearing
a psychological scar of childhood like the one she bore. Ultimately, she
wishes to circumvent for her children anything similar to her own
separation from her mother, an experience whose indelible mark is as
deep as the brand beneath Sethe's mother's breast. We are able to hear
her salient concerns resonating in her reflections of the infamous day:

I wouldn't draw breath without my children . . . My plan was to take us all to
the other side where my own ma'am is . . . You [Beloved] came right on back
like a good girl, like a daughter which is what I wanted to be and would have
been if my ma'am had been able to get out of the rice long enough before they
hanged her and let me be one. . . . I wonder what they was doing when they
was caught. Running, you think? No. Not that. Because she was my ma'am
and nobody's ma'am would run off and leave her daughter would she? (203).

Sethe argues that a mother must and would do anything to ensure the
welfare of her children, even if it means prostituting herself like the
"Saturday girls" who sell their bodies in the slaughterhouse yard.

On the other hand, we must not ignore that Sethe sees her children
as her property; each one is a "life she had made"; each had "all the parts
of her" (163). Thus perceived, Sethe's actions become more complex.
Indeed, she allows us to frame the larger question here that Morrison
seems to have ignored in *Sula:* Does a mother have the right to take the
life of her child? The answer is not cut-and-dried in *Beloved,* especially
since Morrison includes the powerful suggestion, through Sethe's
mother's experience, that the slave child who was born was in fact
wanted by its mother. This, one may argue, leads to the even more
powerful conclusion that "most children born . . . are born as the
realization of the instinctual wishes of their mother."[26]

To be sure, we find in Sethe's behavior yet another example of the slave's resistance to slavery; for though the North American annals of slavery record, relatively speaking, offer few collective and even revolutionary acts of resistance, more were, as Deborah White points out, "generally individualistic, and aimed at maintaining what the slave master and overseer had in the course of their relationships, perceived as acceptable level of work, shelter, force, punishment, and free time . . . the best most could hope for was survival with a modicum of dignity."[27]

More important, although Afro-American lore is replete with male heroic figures, such as High John de Conquer, the paradigmatic trickster, there is ample evidence of his female counterpart, whose creativity successfully undermined the system of slavery. In fact, as White points out, bondswomen, who were as "adept in inventing schemes and excuses to get their own way"[28] as the bondsmen, turned topsy-turvy the system with schemes that ran the gamut from arson and poison to outright murder of the master.

Given the primacy of childbearing to the perpetuation of slavery, however, the bondswoman had, through her reproductive capacity, yet another avenue of resistance; and as records of feigned illness, deliberate and nondeliberate miscarriage, and self-imposed sterility indicate, they found and took advantage of these avenues of resistance. Although infanticide represented, according to White, an "atypical behavior on the part of the slave mothers,"[29] it was nevertheless an avenue that was available and used by some.

Sethe would learn from Nan, a surrogate mother, that her African-born mother had chosen this response. Raped by slave traders and owners, she aborted all resulting pregnancies: "She threw them all away but you. The one from the crew she threw away on the island. The other from more whites she also threw away. Without names, she threw them. You she gave the name of the black man. She put her arms around him. The others she did not put her arms around. Never. Never" (62).

The alternative example was provided by yet another surrogate, Baby Suggs, who had eight children and was forced to part with all but her last son, Halle. For Sethe, it was "simple"—she would put her children "where no one could hurt them" (163). She had shown her propensity to undermine the system of slavery when she succeeded in having a wedding, wedding dress, and honeymoon; and she was now showing the degree of the limitations she would be bound with by killing her daughter, Beloved.

108 TONITONI MORRISON

For Sethe, the dilemma is embodied in the very question of mother-hood, which requires not only that one be "good enough, alert enough, strong enough" but also that one "stay alive just that much longer" (132). Unless a mother remained carefree, she concluded, "mother love was a killer" (132). The complexity of Sethe's rich, ironic statement should not be overlooked. For her, motherlove is, literally and figura-tively speaking, a "killer." Her dilemma emerges essentially from the diametrically opposing views of relationship that the system of slavery demanded and fostered, one grounded in separation of families, and one—sacred to Sethe—grounded in a sense of correctness. Concerned only with its own perpetuation, slavery stood in contradiction to Sethe's ideal of care. She confesses, "I wouldn't draw breath without my chil-dren" (203); and she asks, "nobody's ma'am could run off and leave her daughter, would she?" (203) Clearly, Sethe defines and perceives herself firmly in terms of a world of care and protection for her children.

Like Eva of *Sula,* who rejected the restrictions and condemnation aimed at her by Hannah for killing Plum, Sethe has no interest in Paul D's accusatory remark about her crime:

"Yeah. It didn't work, did it? Did it work?" he asked.
"It worked," she said.
"How? Your boys gone you don't know where. One girl dead, the other won't leave the yard. How did it work?"
"They ain't at Sweet Home. Schoolteacher ain't got 'em."
"Maybe there's worse."
"It ain't my job to know what's worse. It's my job to know what is and to keep them away from what I know is terrible. I did that."
"What you did was wrong, Sethe." (164–65)

Clearly, her intention here is not denial but rationalization; yet, it is rationalization based on conviction.

Sethe is nevertheless held accountable, not only by Paul D but also by the community, Denver, Beloved, and ultimately herself. In part, their apparent objections to Sethe's action emerge from the implica-tions of Sethe's declaration that each of her children is a "life she had made" and that each had "all the parts of her" (163). As her property, Sethe is also saying, she owns her children and has the right to do with them as she pleases.

Be that as it may, Morrison seems here more interested in exploring further the whole issue of ownership. For much in the manner that one must question the Garners' right to own the Sweet Home blacks whom they had purchased, one can find Morrison questioning shades of a similar problem by looking at the issue of parental ownership. The difference is significant, though, because slavery is concerned primarily with economics and the reduction of human beings to chattel for the sake of profit. The other is concerned with what Michael Balint notes is a central aspect of maternal love and may in fact be crucial to what he called "instinctive maternity." According to Balint, "For the mother the child is never grown up, for when grown up he is no longer her child . . . just as the mother is to the child, so is the child to the mother—an object of gratification."[30] Sethe seems to verify this when she says to Beloved, "when I tell you you mine, I also mean I'm yours" (203).

Played out to its fullest, Morrison's implication—one that is clearly supported by the actions of the slave mothers in *Beloved*—is without a doubt that "the child who is born is always the child who is wanted by the mother."[31] But more important, as Morrison also suggested in her other novels, the potential for and absolute power of woman-as-mother must not be gainsaid. Unlike her previous examinations of this subject in the other novels, this is not a closed issue in *Beloved*. Irrespective of Sethe's convictions that it is her job to "know what is," she is not given carte blanche and let off the hook. She is not only taken to jail (a significant irony in the text) but also, and perhaps more important, condemned by the black women in the community, indicted by Denver, abandoned by the man she loves, and haunted by the ghost of the dead child. Above all she is riddled by psychological restlessness.

Together, each response raises not only the whole question of the limitations of motherhood but also that of personal freedom, not merely in the physical sense but essentially in the existential sense, a subject that has concerned Morrison from the beginning in *The Bluest Eye* and one that has concerned us in this study. But whereas heretofore Morrison seemed interested in probing and in fact advocating the importance of her characters' obligation to not act in "bad faith," that is, to act with existential responsibility for self and being, by accepting the challenge of their existential freedom in a chaotic and hostile world, she focuses in *Beloved* on the possible limitations of that freedom as well. For there is here the realization that freedom must fundamentally be viewed in terms of the will to power.

In short, in *Beloved* Morrison does not circumvent, as she seems to have done in the past, what lies at the crux of the whole issue of freedom that we find in her collected works, and that is the realization that ultimately freedom, in the existential sense "actually means the successful subjugation of the will of others"[32] and all of the ramifications of such behavior. Morrison does come close to exploring this subject with Sula. The community never forgives Sula for putting Eva in the rest home, but this anger has to be seen more as disappointment in Sula rather than resentment of her eagerness to harness power. Sula perhaps dies because the untrammeled world she envisioned, one in which individual freedom is sanctioned, is not possible in the end. Morals and values set important (necessary) boundaries.

With slavery as her central trope for the human condition—it represents a universe in which the value of humanity is nonexistent (unless, of course, it is in purely economic terms)—the question of being is amplified by Morrison. But so, too, are the problems of freedom, ethics, and morality in such a world. By having Sethe judged by everyone, from the community to the ghost-child, Morrison inquires, like Sartre, into the whole notion of one achieving a pure existential freedom without interfering with the freedom of the humanity of others. Unlike Sula, who declares to Nel that once such an untrammeled world is achieved "then there'll be a little love left over for me" (*Sula* 146), Sethe discovers the truth: there would be only disgust, not love, in such a world.

Ultimately, then, in *Beloved,* the central question that can be gleaned from Sethe's quest for wholeness is simply this: in her odyssey to freedom, does Sethe have the right/freedom to kill Beloved? Stated differently: is Beloved, although an infant, without her right/freedom to self and being? In other words, by acting as her own god in charting the direction of her life, is Sethe in her role as parent also free to act as god for Beloved, to destroy or deny Beloved's life? Would she have acted in bad faith had she not taken the course of action that she took?

In her escape to physical freedom Sethe had found near selfish pleasure in the love that she bore for her children. She tells Paul D: "Look like I loved 'em more after I got here [Cincinnati and freedom]. Or maybe I couldn't love 'em proper in Kentucky because they wasn't mine to love" (163). But does this boundless freedom and right to love extend infinitely to all areas of life? Paul D suggests that there are limitations: "This here Sethe didn't know where the world stopped and she began" (164). Morrison adds to this muddled response by stating that Sethe did what was right although she did not have the right to do it.[33]

Response to *Beloved*

The deterioration and despair Sethe suffers in the end emerge, in part, from her failure to realize that in acting freely she might have overstepped some boundaries. When the community comes to exorcise Beloved's spirit at the end of the novel, Sethe rises to her defense, much in the way that she had reacted to the coming of schoolteacher twenty years before. Thinking that she must protect her "best thing" (262), Sethe once again can only conclude: "No. no. Nonono," as she charges the intruders with ice pick in hand. Although her response seems almost instinctive, we are left with the frightening realization that Sethe, by trying to destroy the monster that had deprived her and her family of their humanity, had herself become one—much like Richard Wright's Bigger of *Native Son.* Both characters are willing to kill for their beliefs. Thus the obvious complexity of the issues and questions Morrison raises through Sethe makes the tunneled vision and diatribes such as that of Stanley Crouch in his review of *Beloved,* which he calls "a blackface holocaust novel," a sham. Hiding behind a thin veneer of antifeminism, Crouch writes: "Beloved is designed to placate sentimental feminist ideology, and to make sure that the vision of black woman as the most scorned and rebuked of the victims doesn't weaken."[34] Nothing could be further from the truth. Morrison in fact explores humanity without skirting the important questions of race, class, and gender. She does so without being engulfed by them to the degree of operating from a point of ignorance, which is obviously the realm from which Crouch writes.

Because what is at issue is by no means simple, Morrison never ceases to hold before us the environment that created Sethe: economic slavery. It alone remains the source, the context, of her madness—the impetus for her irrational behavior. Interestingly enough, it is Paul D who is able to understand and verbalize Sethe's dilemma. He concludes, "for a used-to-be-slave woman to love anything that much was dangerous, especially if it was her children she had settled on to love" (45). Here Paul D points to the tension created by the system of slavery and the maternal instinct of the slave woman. Slavery claimed ownership of all of its property, irrespective of age and gender, including the siblings of

its female slaves. Simultaneously, the slave mother instinctively sought
to hold on to her progeny.

Communities of Women

Furthermore, in his perceptive remark, Paul D indirectly offers insight into the absence of a significant nurturing factor in Sethe's early
life experiences that made her, like Jadine, a biological and cultural
orphan. Apparently, Sethe had not benefited from what we have called
throughout this study a community of women, for one of the apparent
benefits of such a network is the proper relationship between mother
and child, whether enslaved or free, that would make survival possible.

That such communities existed and in fact were central to women
slaves is verified by Deborah Gray White in her discussion of the
stratification of slave society along gender line. White argues that the
women "had ample opportunity to develop a consciousness grounded in
their identity as females . . . adult female cooperation and interdepen-
dence was a fact of female slave life."[35] White further argues that,

Thus women were put in one another's company for the most of the day. This
meant that those with whom they ate meals, sang work songs, and commiser-
ated during the work day were people with the same kind of responsibilities
and problems. If anything, slave women developed their own female culture,
that is, a way of doing things and a way of assigning value that flowed from the
perspective that they had on Southern plantation life. Rather than being
diminished, their sense of womanhood was probably enhanced, and their
bonds to one another made stronger.[36]

Morrison is certainly not oblivious to such a community, as we see
through brief treatment of Nan, the slave who was closest to Sethe's
mother, as well as the one who served as her surrogate. Nan alone knew
and sought to pass on to Sethe the history of her past, of a mother Sethe
could recall only vaguely, for "she remembered only song and dance.
Not even her own mother, who was pointed out to her by the eight-
year-old child who watched over the young ones—pointed out as the
one among many backs turned away from her, stooping in a watery
field" (30).

But Sethe was a mere child, not even a woman-child at this point,
and for the most part she had forgotten what she had learned from Nan.
"What Nan told her she had forgotten, along with the language she

told it in. The same language her ma'am spoke, and which would never come back" (62).

Without the cultural codes of her womanhood, Sethe is not able to read significant signs of her community, especially after going to Sweet Home where she was the only woman slave. There were no ritual priestesses to guide her through her rite of womanhood, for besides being the slaveholder, Mrs. Garner, the only other woman, was barren. Aunt Phyllis, the midwife, lived on a different plantation and came only when it was time for Sethe to give birth to another child. Consequently, as Sethe would later confess to Paul D, "I wish I'd a known more, but, like I say, there wasn't nobody to talk to. Woman, I mean. . . . It's hard, you know what I mean? by yourself and no woman to help you get through" (160).

The absence of this significant apprenticeship was partly responsible for Sethe's naivete and even the ignorance that allowed her to act "as though Sweet Home really was one" (23). In spite of this, however, and of the fact that the narrator tells us that "A bigger fool never lived" (24), Sethe does reveal that she had attempted at times, especially with reference to her children, "to recollect what I had been back where I was before Sweet Home. How the women did there" (160). In other words, she drew from a vicarious participation in the community of women that existed on the plantation. Furthermore, during the course of the novel, Sethe either enters into or helps to form partnerships in at least four distinct and significant communities of women.

Amy

Sethe forms her first partnership immediately upon embarking on her journey from death to life as she takes flight from schoolteacher, his nephews, Sweet Home, slavery, and Kentucky: "the bloody side of the Ohio River" (31). With a back mutilated by the slaver's whip, breasts raw from the mossy teeth of young violators and thieves, and feet swollen beyond human recognition, Sethe reaches the zenith of her excruciating journey to freedom believing she has reached the threshold of death. Here, she meets Amy, the daughter of a former indentured servant who, like Sethe's mother, had died leaving her offspring to a life of bondage and oppression. Sethe's and Amy's plights are similar in other ways, although Sethe, at nineteen, is the mother of four, while Amy, at eighteen, has never had a child. Both are teenaged women-children, poor, and fugitives. Outsiders, both are searching for a life

away from the liminal world they had known on the other side of the
Ohio River. Sethe is traveling to Cincinnati, Ohio, and her children,
while Amy is on her way to Boston where she hopes to purchase some
velvet.

The subtle differences in the sanctuary and objectives each seeks are
significant, for they point to the crucial distinction that separates the
two voyagers: though they are of the same gender, they are racially
different; one is black, the other white. Amy is without children at
eighteen because she was not considered a human reproduction machine, the producer of a labor force. She can in fact seek a more
materialistic quality of life, and even one housed in the very nucleus of
her culture, western culture, symbolized by both the velvet she knows
she can have and her destination: Boston, the Edenic "city upon a hill"
that lies at the foundation of American intellectual and cultural life.
But Sethe is not afforded such luxury. She is not only a black woman
but a black slave woman; above all, she is the mother of black slave
children. Thus freedom for Sethe necessarily involves not only her
physical and psychological liberation but also the welfare of her children. Culture for her is not as accessible, for although she can recall the
song and the dance of her mother's generation, she cannot remember
her native tongue, the language spoken by them. The American dream
for her can only be a nightmare, a chokecherry tree that grows on her
back. Because she cannot return to her cultural roots, to Africa, freedom must become her "errand into the wilderness," her symbolic flight
to a mythical "city on a hill."

Consequently, though both women are runaways, Amy does not have
to conceal her identity. Her race alone gives her a freedom of movement
that Sethe cannot experience. Amy can travel by day, open and visible,
without the need of a pass, without restriction. Though she is, according to Sethe, "the raggediest looking [poor white] trash you ever saw"
(31–32), Amy can walk upright during the lap of their brief pilgrimage together. Sethe must literally and figuratively crawl on her hands
and knees, although she is six months pregnant and seriously injured.
Unlike Amy, who identifies herself as "Miss Amy Denver" while per-
ceiving Sethe as no more than a "nigger woman," Sethe must live in
fear, concealing her real identity from even her travel mate, whom she
tells to call her "Lu." "However far she was from Sweet Home, there
was no point in giving out her real name to the first person she saw"
(33–34).

Irrespective of these differences, there is almost immediate bonding between these two perfect strangers, as well as a level of communication that seems almost intuitive. "They did not look directly at each other, nor straight into the eyes anyway. Yet they slipped effortlessly into yard chat about nothing in particular" (33). To be sure, Amy cannot abrogate, during their brief encounter, her socialized view of "Lu," who to her could be no more than a "nigger woman"; but she nevertheless seems able to circumvent it when, during this "yard chat," she finds a common ground that allows her to challenge Sethe to not surrender her life to death. Amy asks, "What you going to do, just lay there and foal?" Clearly, Amy's socialization dominates her thought, for she sees Sethe, on the one hand, as no more than a pregnant animal who is about to give birth. On the other hand, though, she seems taken by Sethe's determination and drive, and she consequently challenges her to not relinquish what has apparently been a valiant struggle for survival.

That this is nevertheless a sororal relationship is made evident by the key metaphor "yard chat," which suggests communal dialogue and oneness. Once one enters another's "yard," traditional barriers are crossed and often suspended; fences are removed, gates are opened, and relationships established. We see this in Amy's evolving roles; from stranger to nurse, midwife, and finally friend. With her assistance Sethe is able to embark on the road to recovery. Finding sanctuary in an abandoned lean-to, Amy begins Sethe's restoration by massaging her swollen feet "until she cried salt tears," assuring Sethe that "anything dead coming back to life hurts" (35). Amy's role as resurrectress is more evident in her treatment of Sethe's back, whose labyrinthine scars are testimonials to her oppression. Although the tree Amy sees in the scars must be perceived as a "tree of life"—as a symbol of Sethe's history—it is also a symbol of the cross or burden she bears. Discovering Sethe's disfigured back and the pain that emanates from the branches, Amy, with the organic and herbal skills of Milkman's Aunt Pilate, continues her curative role. Turning to nature, in the tradition of the *curandera* that she is, Amy gathers "two palmfuls of [spider] web, which she cleaned of prey and then draped on Sethe's back, saying it was like stringing a tree for Christmas" (80).

Above all, it is Amy's role as midwife that bonds the women together, although briefly. Sethe is able to give birth to her premature baby girl, Denver, and the child is able to live because Amy is there to assist her. When Sethe goes into labor immediately upon reaching the Ohio River, she has to depend upon the strong hands of her teenaged companion woman-child, for the baby was "face up and drowning in its mother's blood." Discarding any hope in anyone other than herself, "Amy stopped begging Jesus" and with her "strong hands went to work." This special, almost instinctive response serves to cement the two "throw away people, two lawless outlaws—a slave and a barefoot white woman with unpinned hair" together (84). Though by no means superficial, the bond between them is tenuous; for although united by gender, they are not bonded by race, a factor that looms like an invisible wall between Sethe, the former slave, and Amy, a "barefoot whitewoman." Not surprisingly, Amy resolved that "she wouldn't be caught dead in daylight on a busy river with a runaway" (85). Leaving, she insisted that Sethe eventually tell her baby daughter that "Miss Amy Denver," of Boston, had helped to bring her into this world.

Thus, although Amy and Sethe form an important community of women, its significance is diminished in part by the fact that its genesis was a matter of expediency. Although their relationship resonates with images of the classic friendship developed between Jim and Huck in Twain's *The Adventures of Huckleberry Finn,* one never senses that Amy achieves the level of respect for Sethe that Huck achieves for Jim. There is no sense of reciprocity here. The fact remains, however, that Amy, a name that interestingly enough means friend or beloved, stops, assists, protects, and helps to heal Sethe. She could easily have journeyed on, or certainly turned in the fugitive Sethe. She does neither one.

Baby Suggs

Equally significant is the healing that Sethe experiences in yet another federation with women, specifically the one she encounters upon her arrival at 124 Bluestone Road. In many ways, it signalled her continued resurrection, her ascendance into a world reigned over by yet another Morrisonian earth mother, "Baby Suggs, holy," Sethe's mother-in-law who, though left physically and emotionally handicapped by slave life, knew how to dance in the sunlight (86).

The initial contact is as tenuous as Sethe's union with Amy. We note, too, that the structure of this relationship is not the traditional Morrisonian triad, such as that found in *Sula* and *Song of Solomon.* Nevertheless, at 124 Sethe finds a sanctuary established by Baby Suggs, holy, who after sixty years of enslavement had her freedom bought by her son Halle, Sethe's husband. Although her life at Sweet Home had been relatively atypical, for while there "nobody, but nobody knocked her down" (139), and although she even questioned the need for freedom at her age, Baby Suggs discovered upon crossing the Ohio "that there was nothing like [freedom] in the world" (141). Most important, Baby Suggs's newfound freedom had allowed her to discover her own heartbeat and to occupy her time at 124 "giving advice; passing messages; healing the sick, hiding fugitives, loving, cooking, cooking, loving, preaching, singing, dancing and loving everybody like it was her job and hers alone" (137).

Thus, although she arrives as 124 "all mashed up and slit open" (135), for the first time in her life Sethe is able to claim herself with Baby Suggs's assistance. Not only does she have women friends, but she encounters days of healing under the skillful hands of her mother-in-law, who "bathed her in sections, wrapped her womb, combed her hair, oiled her nipples, stitched her clothes, cleaned her feet, greased her back" (98). An "uncalled, unrobed, and unanointed preacher" (87) and healer, Baby Suggs offered her great big heart, in a manner similar to Amy's offering of her strong hands. It took both, the rational (Amy) and the emotive (Suggs) to enhance Sethe's journey to recovery and self. Both make a difference in Sethe's life.

Above all, it is through Baby Suggs, holy, that Sethe is able to garner the ultimate, exhilarating experience of community, for Baby Suggs alone leads her to the ritual grounds of the clearing where, as ritual priestess, she conducts the rite of cleansing that leads Sethe to the catharsis she needs and allows her to transcend her liminality. Ritual grounds, as Robert Stepto explains, "offer the exhilarating prospect of community, protection, progress, learning and religion."[37] The clearing is without a doubt such a place. Here, although she would summon the children to laugh and men to dance, Baby Suggs, holy, would command the women to "Cry . . . For the living and the dead. Just cry" (88). At the end of this rejuvenation ritual, in which the women would eventually stop crying and dance, Baby Suggs's words were sacramental, for she "told them that the only grace they could have was the grace they could imagine" (88). Above all, she implored them to realize and accept the value of self-love as the only true vehicle to rebirth: "Here," she said, "in this here place, we flesh; flesh that weeps, laughs; flesh that dances on bare feet in grass. Love it. Love it hard. . . . More than lungs that have yet to draw free air. More than your life-holding womb and your life-giving parts, hear me now, love your heart. For this is the prize" (88–89). Specifically for Sethe, Baby Suggs was a reassuring and encouraging voice that admonished her to abandon her burdens: "Lay em down, Sethe. Sword and shield. Down.

TONI MORRISON

Down. Both of 'em down. Down by the riverside. Sword and shield. Don't study war no more. Lay all that mess down" (86).

Before her past of misery reappears in the form of schoolteacher, Sethe experiences an unprecedented twenty-eight days of freedom at 124 Bluestone Road. Equated with a lunar month, with "the travels of one whole moon" (95), this period of Sethe's "unslaved life" (95) is of paramount importance; for like the lunar cycle to which the narrator alludes, it signifies a period of regeneration and renewal—of life, death, and rebirth. Similarly, like the menstrual cycle to which it also inevitably alludes given Sethe's central role as great mother, it symbolizes a period of promised new life, fertility, and gestation followed by death. Prefigured here is not only the flow of blood that takes place at the end of the cycle with the aborted ovum, but also the bloody scene that will take place at the moment that Sethe will once again lose her freedom, her own symbolic death, as well as the blood that will flow from the slain Beloved, whose life is abruptly aborted. Although it ends tragically for Sethe, this twenty-eight day period accords her "days of healing, ease, and real talk" (95), as well as "days of having women friends, mother-in-law, and all her children together" (173). Thus, it brings regeneration and stability, allowing Sethe to exit the orbit of her liminal world of slavery though she is still legally a slave; she is fugitive.

Significantly, Sethe's aggregation goes beyond mother-in-law, children, and women friends to the community at large. This brief experience also offers her days "of being part of a neighborhood, of in fact having neighbors at all to call her own" (173). Morrison emphasizes here the significance of place, much in the manner that she had done with the Bottom in *Sula* and Not Doctor Street in *Song of Solomon*. But she goes beyond the mere identification of place to the actual grounding of Sethe in a specific community. Thus Sethe is able to transcend her marginality through the act of "groundation," in short, through her incorporation into a community of women and into a community at large (a neighborhood). She thereby achieves a dimension of identity that Sula rejected but Milkman accepted.

The necessity and significance of this act of bonding is to be found in the initiation rite that Baby Suggs, holy, conducts for Sethe with her communal feast for ninety who "ate so well, and laughed so much": "Baby Suggs' three (maybe fours) pies grew to ten (maybe twelve). Sethe's two hens became five turkeys. The one block of ice brought all the way from Cincinnati—over which they poured mashed watermelon mixed with sugar and mint to make a punch—became a wagonload of ice cakes for a washtub full of strawberry shrug. 124 rock[ed] with laughter, goodwill, and food for ninety" (137). Added to this was Stamp Paid's meal-fried perch, corn pudding made with cream, and roasted rabbit.

Although Baby Suggs's Christ-like act is clearly a biblical allusion to Jesus' feeding the multitude with the two fish and five loaves of bread, one can find in her actions the fulfillment of her priestly responsibilities, a role that relates her to Pilate of *Song of Solomon*. The gathering becomes in fact a confirmation ceremony, which on the one hand adopts Sethe into the community and on the other crystallizes and guards further the community's extant sense of self against those who, unable to understand the display of communal unity and love, were furious with disapproval. Although formerly without a structured self in slavery, Sethe was no longer outsider, or transitional being. The total experience allows her to continue her metamorphosis to center and self, her ultimate journey. "Freeing yourself was one thing; claiming ownership of that freed self was another" (95).

Schoolteacher's appearance signals the completion of the lunar cycle—full moon or death; it brings to fruition Sethe's "short-lived glory" (173). It is, to be sure, her symbolic death, for if schoolteacher's purpose is carried out she will once again possess the status of chattel, property to be returned to Sweet Home and Kentucky. Also, it is the precipitation of the physical death of Beloved, Sethe's "best thing"; significantly, it is also the demise and dissolution of the allies and federations she had established. In the end, Sethe's brutal act of murder becomes a ritually polluting agent and ceremony that sullies her salient relations with Baby Suggs, holy, and the community at large, and her community of women.

The outcome is disastrous. Baby Suggs abandons all hope of life and resigns herself to death, contemplating colors as she does, after the ghost-child's visitations become abusive: "The heart that pumped out love, the mouth that spoke the Word, didn't count. They came in her yard anyway and she could not approve or condemn Sethe's rough choice. One or the other might have saved her, but beaten up by the claims of both, she went to bed" (180). Baby Suggs went to bed to "lay it all down, sword and shield" for good; "her big old heart quit" (104).

Similarly, the community stepped "back and [held] itself at a distance" (177), ostracizing Sethe and ignoring her presence in its midst. Initially, the community gathered to support her, even if no more than with a "cape of sound" to wrap around her, "like arms to hold and

steady her on her way" (152). They were soon taken aback, however, by
what appeared to be Sethe's lack of remorse: "Was her head a bit too
high? Her back a little too straight?" (152). Eventually, "Just about
everybody in town was longing for Sethe to come on difficult times.
Her outrageous claims, her self-sufficiency seemed to demand it" (171).
After Baby Suggs's death, "Nobody, but nobody visited that house"
(184). Her twenty-eight days of freedom was replaced with "eighteen
years of disapproval and solitary life" (173).

It is significant, however, that once the women of the community
are apprised of Beloved's physical return and parasitic relation with
Sethe, they act to exorcise her. Like the women who gathered at Aunt
Jimmy's funeral in *The Bluest Eye,* they come together to conduct the
appropriate ritual of affirmation for a member of their group. For them,
Beloved's physical presence is an invasion. They consider Beloved's
presence evil, more profane than Sethe's original act. Convinced, nevertheless, that "the past [was] something to leave behind," (256), thirty
women embark on the necessary purification ritual to cleanse 124
Bluestone Road and the community once and for all of Sethe's original
sin.

More important, in ceremonies that are reminiscent of Baby Suggs's
rituals in the clearing, they purge the community of the pollutant, the
"unleashed and sassy" (256) sin that had intruded in the form of Beloved. Beloved is to be warded off and not tolerated, unlike Sula, who,
though considered evil, was allowed to strive by the Bottomites, who
used her as a scapegoat. Unlike the people of the Bottom, who act and
feel impotent, Sethe's community of women rally to destroy the intruder. "Building voice upon voice until they found it, and when they
did it was a wave of sound wide enough to sound deep water and knock
the pods off chestnut trees. It broke over Sethe and she trembled like
the baptized in its wash" (261). Cleansed, Sethe is made ready for
aggregation; the communal doors are once again opened to her.

Sethe and Her Daughters

It is possible to argue that the most tragic result of Sethe's heinous
crime is the damage that it does to the single most important community of women to her: the community she forms with her daughters,
Beloved and Denver. With Sethe's perennial sense of guilt, Denver's
sense of alienation, and Beloved's need for retribution, their unity
remains superficial, in spite of the external evidences to the contrary.

Each response forms a wedge that widens the existing fissure in their superficial bond. In the end they have only the shadow of the "sunsplashed life" (173) Sethe is convinced is reflected in the "hand-holding shadows" she sees on her way back from the carnival.

Although she attempts to muster evidence of the inseparability of the three of them ("us three"), we find support for the opposite. One scene, in particular, involving Sethe, Denver, and Beloved, serves as an excellent example: deciding to accept the severity of her fate, Sethe attempts to briefly transcend the junkheap she has been dumped on by turning toward her children. When Beloved discovers some old skates in the house, Sethe decides that all three will go ice skating on the frozen creek. The scene is, without a doubt, one of the most sensitively drawn episodes in the novel. Poetically alive, metaphorically rich, and structurally unified, it is a clear illustration of Morrison's artistic ability, her sense of craft. Unified by the simple refrain, "Nobody saw them falling" (174), the passage allows us to capture the momentum of the uncontrolled turbulence of their relationship as it rollercoasters under the impetus of forces over which they seem to have no control. In their movement together one finds embedded and echoed a synopsis of their individual struggle—of their futile effort to stand level footed in their world. While Beloved skates with two skates and Denver skates with one, Sethe has only shoe slides, "but nobody saw them falling":

Holding hands, bracing each other, they swirled over the ice. Beloved wore the pair; Denver wore one, step-gliding over the treacherous ice. Sethe thought her two shoes would hold and anchor her. She was wrong. Two paces onto the creek, she lost her balance and landed on her behind. The girls, screaming with laughter, joined her on the ice. Sethe struggled to stand and discovered not only that she could do a split, but that it hurt. Her bones surfaced in unexpected places and so did laughter. Making a circle or a line, the three of them could not stay upright for one whole minute, but nobody saw them falling. (174)

Efforts to support one another are futile; tumbling, "Their skirts flew like wings and their skin turned pewter in the cold and dying light." Drained by the experience, "they lay on their backs to recover breath . . . Winter stars, close enough to lick, had come out before sunset" (174).

Images of unity abound here. The three women hold hands, attempt to protect one another, skate in circles, laugh, fall, and cry together.

They appear, at this instant, to be self-sufficient. It mattered not that they were closed out from the world around them—that "nobody saw them falling"—for they have one another. It is crucial, however, that the images of unity and wholeness that seem to dominate are subsumed by powerful images of death, the most important of which is the frozen creek on which they skate.

With her use of the creek, Morrison returns to the recurring water metaphor that dominates *Beloved;* and as in almost all previous instances this central element is closely associated with Sethe. When seen before, however, the association between water and life, new life, and rebirth was clear. Water was perceived as aqua vitae; it was the river of life. For example, this association can be made between Sethe and the Ohio River. Once she crosses it to the land of freedom she has new life; once she sees the Ohio River her water breaks and she gives birth to Denver. She drinks water from the Ohio, a form of ritual cleansing, and Baby Suggs bathes her, providing the ritual purification (rebirth) that she needs to enter the new community. Beloved, her dead child, returns by walking out of the water; and immediately upon seeing Beloved, Sethe experiences an artificial delivery, symbolized by a bladder that spilled before she could get to the outhouse. Significantly, she thinks the endless turret of water is similar to the "flooding" that took place at the time of Denver's birth.

In contrast to the common references to water as a life-giving source, in the ice skating scene the water, though present, is frozen. The creek, a tributary to the river, is dormant, without life—dead in the midst of winter. Thus, in spite of the jubilation, images of death abound. This is not a "sunsplashed life" shared by "us three," but instead a period where "winter stars, close enough to lick had come out before sunset" (174). The premature completion of their day relates directly to the incomplete nature of their relationship together. One might even argue that the "soul" has been removed from their unified body, as might be suggested by the shadows that Sethe claims represented them and by the pewter that is associated with their complexion. Ultimately, however, the paucity of the community that they form is embodied in Sethe's final action. Returning home, she feeds the girls warm milk, to which she has had to add syrup and vanilla. Irony lies not in the fact that she would feed them milk, for as nurse and nurturer, that is her responsibility. Significantly, it is not her milk that she feeds them, for it had been polluted by schoolteacher's nephews and Beloved's blood; it had turned to the clabber like that with which Halle had rubbed his face. She can, to a large degree, only offer them milk that is now artificially flavored.

Paul D

Paradoxically, the "sunsplashed life" that offers Sethe the greatest satisfaction is the byproduct of her relationship with Paul D, "the last of the Sweet Home men," who brings her unfathomable joy, allowing her to once again feel alive. Morrison's treatment of her males and the male-female relationship theme in *Beloved* is unparalleled in her collected work. Here the males are most complex—there are no flying Africans or Boy-Boys who abandon families, no Jude Greens who cannot be faithful to their wives, no Ajaxes or Milkmen who take flight from what they consider possessive love.

Even when underdeveloped, the male characters for the most part are rich with admirable qualities. For example, though himself a slave, Morrison's Halle purchases his mother's freedom with his own life, Six-O walks miles to maintain a meaningful relationship with a woman slave on a distant plantation, Stamp Paid makes the ultimate sacrifice out of respect for the woman he loves, and Paul D, who comes in search of Sethe, promises her: "Sethe, if I'm here with you, with Denver, you can go anywhere you want. Jump, if you want to 'cause I'll catch you girl. I'll catch you 'fore you fall. Go as far inside as you need to, I'll hold your ankles. Make sure you get back out" (46). Throughout the text Paul D's actions prove that his are not empty words, in spite of his human frailties, and in spite of his life experiences, which for the most part have been as horrendous as Sethe's. He is unique in Morrison's canon, but so is the relationship that he seeks to develop with Sethe.

At the point of finding Sethe, Paul D's intentions appear, to a large degree, to be purely sexual. One feels that the meeting provides an opportunity for him to display his manhood in a manner heretofore unwitnessed by Sethe. For not only had she been made an object of sexual desire for him and the other Sweet Home men who had wasted themselves on cows while waiting for her to choose from among them, but she had also chosen someone else and witnessed his deterioration as well under schoolteacher's brutal management. Their first sexual encounter, however, results in premature ejaculation. Nevertheless, Paul D remains; he does not follow the pattern of Ajax and Milkman, who abandon their lovers.

Thus, it also must be said that Paul D's concern at this point emerges from more than mere questions of sexual prowess or physical wholeness, for although *Beloved* is Sethe's story and, as noted above, thematically and structurally her slave narrative, it is also Paul D's record of his quest for self, for authentic existence. Consequently, multi-faceted and distinct phases of his metaphoric and symbolic births, deaths, and rebirths are evidenced.

Eminently important in his quest for physical wholeness is not only the altruistic manner in which he had been treated by Mr. Garner, to whom all the male slaves were "men everyone of them" (10); perhaps more important, is the devastating manner in which he was later physically and psychologically emasculated by schoolteacher. For whereas Garner had sought to develop men, schoolteacher had been more interested in breaking in children. These diametrically distinct treatments created an internal turbulence of opposing movements in Paul D's life, with an epicenter that was fueled by tensions that propelled him forward.

The dissimilarity in these objectives is inherent in the symbolism of the rifles Garner provided for his male slaves and that are immediately expropriated by schoolteacher. Significantly, when Paul D's escape from slavery is foiled, he is captured by rifle- and lamp-carrying whites, both men and boys. One is immediately reminded of the rifle- and lamp-carrying hunters who intrude upon Cholly's first sexual initiation in *The Bluest Eye* and of the resulting psychological castration and damage that would not only last a lifetime for him but that lie at the core of his vicious raping of his daughter. Whereas the phallic rifles symbolize the denied and lost manhood of the slaves, the lamp undoubtedly symbolically sheds light on the path of life of emasculation to which both Paul D and Cholly are heir. Indeed, the lamp carried by the hunters in *The Bluest Eye* casts a beam that leads retrospectively to the historical genesis of this legacy, one that was deeply rooted in the physionomistic convictions of schoolteacher, the leader of the capturers (hunters), who assessed and measured human personality according to physical indices, in this case race.

It is through Mister, however, "the smiling boss of roosters" (108) of the Sweet Home plantation, that Morrison offers her most poignant and effective metaphor for and symbol of Paul D's sense of powerlessness and liminality. After he is captured Paul D realizes his ultimate degradation and dehumanization. He is reduced to chattel when his feet are shackled, a three-spoke collar laced around his neck, and a bit placed in his mouth before he is tethered to a buckboard (notice the pun) and taken to be sold away from Sweet Home. En route from the plantation grounds he encounters Mister, whose life, ironically, Paul D had saved at birth. Prancing with seemingly unfathomable self-pride, Mister, whose comb Paul D confesses is "as big as my hand and some kind of red" (72), becomes a source of humiliation for him. Despite the obvious sexual connotations, related most often to prowess, especially in blues lyrics, but ironically to the theme of emasculation here, what goads Paul D is the fact that "Mister . . . looked so . . . free" (72). One senses that Paul D realizes that the significant respect accorded the pugilistic cock, who could "whup everything in the yard" (72), would never be bestowed on him; both figuratively and literally he would never be a "Mister." The deference associated with the mere mention of the rooster's name is absent from any address to Paul D. Biblically, Paul denotes small; moreover, Paul D lacks a surname—that is, history and family—and must share his first name with two brothers, implying anonymity. Paul D perceptively declares: "Mister was allowed to be and stay what he was. But I wasn't . . . I was something else and that something was less than a chicken sittin in the sun on a tub" (72).

The apotheosis of Paul D's dehumanization, however, comes with yet another experience of enslavement: the eighty-six days of shackled existence he would spend on a chain gang in Alfred, Georgia, where he had been sent after attempting to kill Brandywine, his new owner. If his former (and earlier) experience at Sweet Home with the Garners can be considered Edenic in any way, a "cradle," as he would later call it, then the opposite is true of his Alfred experience. Here his daily life was a *totentaz,* a death (chain) dance that ended in his symbolic entombment in a wooden prison at the end of each day, one that "drove him crazy so he would not lose his mind" (40).

While in Alfred, "Life was dead. Paul D beat her butt all day every day till there was no whimper in her" (109). Nevertheless, his determination to achieve self-affirmation is neither abated nor destroyed but is in fact most visible, both in his continual effort to escape from slavery and in his symbolic resurrection and rebirth from his wooden grave. The opportunity to escape comes during a torrential rain that converts his wooden tomb into a watery grave, when the earth surrounding the trenches encasing his prison begins to dissolve into muddy waters that seep into the boxes: "The water was above [Paul D's] ankles, flowing over the wooden plank he slept on. . . . The mud was up to his thighs and he held on to the bars . . . One by one from Hi Man [the leader] back on down the line, they dove. Down through the mud under the

bars, blind, groping . . ." (110). With desperate comrades Paul D
demonstrates both his resolution and determination at this juncture to
recapture his life, evincing, like Milkman of *Song of Solomon,* a willingness to accept responsibility for self. In short, what we see is Paul D
acting here to will his own existence, to achieve being and essence in a
world of absolute nothingness.

We see, too, Morrison's return to her propensity to turn topsy-turvy
the world in which her characters must live to find meaning and
wholeness. We find here as well allusions to the now familiar phoenix
metaphor that was also present in *Sula* and *Song of Solomon.* In short,
Paul D's watery grave, like Plum's conflagrated place of rest and Milkman's leap, becomes a nurturing womb. Here again the crucial vehicle
and component is nature, in general, but specifically one of the four
elements which remain in Morrison's canon central avenues of rebirth:
fire in *Sula,* air in *Song of Solomon,* and water and earth in *Beloved.*
Significantly missing at this point in Paul D's regeneration, however, is
the surrogate in the form of a mother goddess such as Eva, or great
mother such as Pilate. Literally and figuratively speaking, nature becomes mother: earth (as) mother, who ministers to Paul D. Unlike
Milkman, whose identity is insulated in the lore of the flying African,
and unlike Son, whose cultural roots incubate in Eloe, Paul D remains
without history or family. "Mother. Father. Didn't remember one.
Never saw the other" (49). Muddied with water, earth becomes the clay
from which Paul D must fashion himself anew; he must emerge to
breathe new life and shape himself. (It might be argued, however, that
later Sethe would become such a figure for him.)

Equally significant is what one might perceive as a community of
men in *Beloved,* for the chains bond the men together, demanding both
unity and uniformity in their efforts to survive. Paul D's success is
dependent upon the solidarity of the entire group, "For one lost all lost.
The chain that held them would save all or none" (110). Thus, this
body of men is unlike the Seven Days of *Song of Solomon,* whose objectives seem more destructive than creative, as indicated by Guitar's
revengeful attack against Milkman at the end. Moreover, although
mud and water combine to convey images of death in *Beloved,* as in the
frozen pond on which Sethe skates with her daughters, the dominant
movement of the men is upward. They do not fall but rise, in images
that suggest physical resurrection. Later, when sanctuary-offering
Cherokees remove the men's chains and give them mush, the former
gang members experience a final ritual of rebirth and cleansing, symbol-

ized by the broken chains and the continuously falling rain that washes them in flight.

Because Paul D's journey north to Delaware and eventually to Ohio and Sethe is part of his journey to physical wholeness, authentic existence, and self, it is inevitable that his is also a journey to psychological wholeness and spiritual self. Along with the rifles, schoolteacher had denied the Sweet Home men their thoughts, condemning them as "trespassers among the human race" (125). Battered from the transformation to chattel, Paul D became callous. Paradoxically, schoolteacher had done this at the point in Paul D's life when, irrespective of his status as slave, he was at "the peak of his strength, taller than tall men and stronger than most" (220). But it was the devastation caused by the loss of friends, who formed his surrogate family, providing a "cradle" for him at Sweet Home, that caused Paul D to harden his heart. In its place he kept a "tobacco tin buried in his chest . . . Its lid rusted shut" (72–73), as a means, like Sethe, of "beating back the past." The meaning of family to Paul D thus provides the most significant insight into his quest for psychological wholeness and spiritual self.

Although he confesses to being a wanderer—a "walking man"—Paul D is careful to inform Sethe that this does not mean he had been a mere vagrant. All along he had traveled with a particular direction in mind, one that would lead him directly to her. He tells her, "But when I got here and sat out there on the porch, waiting for you, well, I knew it wasn't the place I was heading toward; it was you." Indeed, he seems convinced that together they could create a meaningful existence. He declares: "We can make a life, girl. A life" (46). Paul D's discourse in both instances reveals a primordial element in his spiritual and psychological quest: his desire for family. Not surprisingly, this interest appears at times to collide head-on with a vanity and egocentrism (call it a "Mister" complex) that emerge from his own insecurity about lost manhood and from the fact that he has never had a family. This seems particularly true when he tells Sethe: "I want you pregnant" (128), without offering any clear explanation.

In spite of this, however, even a cursory examination of the text provides sufficient evidence that Paul D is not merely seeking documentation of his manhood. Examples abound, such as his promise to catch Sethe if she should fall, the pure ecstasy he experiences with Sethe and Denver at the carnival, and his expulsion of the spirit child from 124 Bluestone Road. "She [Sethe] got enough without you. She got enough!" (18), he shouts as he banishes the intruder. Though this act can be seen as a reassertion of manhood, it also reveals Paul D's interest in protecting Sethe. Protection is a significant responsibility in the life of a family, a unit that remains an elusive luxury for the former slave. Yet family remains an integral to him, especially after the fragmentation and subsequent loss of his Sweet Home family: "Once, in Maryland, he met four families of slaves who had all been together for a hundred years: great-grands, grands, mothers, fathers, aunts, uncles, cousins, children . . . He watched them with awe and envy, and each time he discovered large families of black people he made them identify over and over who each was, what relation, who, in fact, belonged to who" (219). Paul D had no memory of any such tangible roots.

Although Sethe had been his initial hope to begin a family, she had chosen a different spouse. Moreover, schoolteacher's symbolic castration had also signified the loss of any opportunity for the Sweet Home men to assume the kind of credible duty to care and provide for, as well as protect (they had no weapons), a family. Paul D is painfully aware that this sense of impotence in the final analysis is what drove Halle insane as he watched helplessly while Sethe's milk was taken by schoolteacher's assaulting nephews. "It broke him," Paul D explained. "A man ain't a goddam ax . . . Things get to him. Things he can't chop down because they're inside" (69). He is also able to discern the similarity of their plight by understanding the significance of the bit that had been placed in his mouth to designate his own voicelessness, helplessness, and impotence. More important, Paul D comes to appreciate the heroism and victory Six-O achieved in laughing, though he was tied to a tree, shot, and burnt. Six-O had died laughing knowing that Seven-O, "his blossoming seed" (229), had escaped with its mother, to experience a physical freedom not known by its father. In a manner of speaking, Six-O assumed the ultimate responsibility for family. He sacrificed himself for their escape and safety.

In the end, theoretically speaking, finding Sethe after twenty-five years of search gives Paul D the opportunity to achieve his desired but still allusive goal of a family. Ultimately, then, it is within the context of the significance of family to Paul D that his initial, brutal rejection of Sethe when he learns about her heinous crime must be understood. Unable to accept what he perceived as Sethe's poor rationalization of "safety with a handsaw" (164), he retorts with an insult allusive to schoolteacher's sentiments—"You got two feet, Sethe, not four" (165)—before abandoning her. Undoubtedly, Paul D's insensitivity and wounding remark emerge not only from his shattered idealization of Sethe but also from the implications of her actions for his dreams. Once again, he seems convinced, her independent action indirectly led to the abortion of his dream of a family. He had gone to Ohio to find "a girl he used to know" (270), but found, he concludes, someone else. Consequently, his apparent inability to separate his sense of manhood from his love for Sethe is destructive to their relationship.

The tension between Paul D's male vanity and his sincere love for Sethe, both of which appear quite natural and realistic, is present from their first reunion. Prior to their first lovemaking, he takes Sethe's breasts in hand while caressing her scarred back with his face:

Behind her, bending down, his body an arc of kindness, he held her breasts in the palms of his hands. He rubbed his cheek on her back and learned that way her sorrow, the roots of it; its wide trunk and intricate branches . . . he saw the sculpture her back had become . . . he could think but not say, "Aw, Lord, girl." And he would tolerate no peace until he had touched every ridge and leave of it with his mouth. (17–18)

This poignantly tender moment offers, without a doubt, a concrete example of the depth of Paul D's love for Sethe. Though unproven, it can not be considered superficial because of his apparent idealization. His "gesture of tenderness" (26) in fact provides Sethe with yet another ritual of rejuvenation akin to those performed by Amy and Baby Suggs, for it allows her the experience of laying down her burdens, as Baby Suggs had insisted she should. "What [Sethe] knew was that the responsibility for her breasts, at last, was in someone else's hand" (18).

Paul D's tender caress must thus be perceived not merely as eros but pathos as well. It is grounded in his realization, acceptance, and celebration of her role as nurturer; for the breasts that he cradles in his hands are the symbols of fertility and motherhood that we come to identify with Sethe throughout the text. She tells Paul D: "I was pregnant with Denver but I had milk for my baby girl" (16). The tree on her back that he kisses records the history of her fertility, her commitment to motherhood (nurturer), and the consequences she had borne for it. Together, the tree and breasts are symbols that promise the realization of Paul D's dream of a family; Sethe's fertile breasts would have milk for his offspring, but the dream would be shattered by the revelation of her crime. It is, however, his repugnant response following their lovemaking, in which he faces with disgust the reality of her sagging breasts and revolting scars, as well as his inability to accept the fact that

Sethe had survived without assistance from him or Halle, that reveals
his internal tensions, ones that lie deep in a male psyche and self-esteem
that had been affected by his life in Kentucky and Georgia. Unlike
Sethe's visible scars, which did not impede her loving with a love that
was "too thick," Paul D's rusted tobacco can made jagged the diastolic
and systolic movements of his frozen heart. Not surprisingly, he sings
blues songs that, "like flat headed nails for pounding and pounding"
(40), reflect the chaos within.

Irrespective of his egocentric behavior and the territorial battles
waged by him over Sethe with Beloved from the beginning (her strate-
gies included his seduction), Paul D, who "anything could stir" (268),
who "could walk into a house and make women cry" and could not
conceal that there was "something blessed in his manner" (17), would
in many ways form the very fulcrum on which her life would balance,
just as he had promised, as she struggles to propel herself toward her
own authentic existence.

Ultimately, we are left with the celebration of a relationship that
transcends interferences, internal and external, and that triumphs,
based on a reciprocity firmly grounded in love, trust, commitment,
and support. Paul D suggests as much when he asks Sethe to realize
that he was not interested in interfering with her relationship with her
daughters but in having her make "some space" for him (45). His
actions on two specific occasions ultimately bear this out.

In the first instance, he and Sethe get caught in the snow together
when Paul D goes to her place of employment to walk her home.
Although he had gone there in part to tell her about the intimacy he
had shared with Beloved, Paul D asks Sethe to bear his child instead.
Thinking that he could not be serious and feeling frightened but flat-
tered, Sethe converts the tone of the moment into one of gaiety that
leaves them holding hands, kissing, and laughing like young lovers lost
in a brisk winter wind. "Man you make me feel like a girl . . . Nobody
ever did that before" (127), Sethe confesses. While they stand locked in
each other's embrace, "not breathing, not even caring if a passerby
passed them by," snow begins to fall, "like a present come down from
the sky" (129). Although both perceive the snow as a blessing from
above, Paul encourages Sethe to run toward the house, as he jovially
pulls his resisting mate along:

"Stop! Stop!" she said. "I don't have the legs for this."
"Then give 'em to me," he said and before she knew it he had backed into

her, hoisted her on his back and was running down the road past brown fields turning white." (130)

Because of the significance of play here, one hears echoes of the ice skating scene shared by Sethe, Denver, and Beloved. Again, there are rich and vibrant metaphors, images of unity and oneness, and language rich with the commitment of support. Much in the manner that the women hold hands and skate in a circle, defending themselves against the external world, Paul D and Sethe hold hands and embrace. There are, however, significant differences. Though nobody sees the women falling, defenseless against gravity and the frozen ice, they fall nevertheless. In contrast, Paul D suggests that Sethe need not worry about falling, that she can stand with him as her support. In sum, he willingly offers to sacrifice himself, circumventing any chance that Sethe would encounter danger. More important, he symbolically assumes responsibility for her by hoisting her onto his back, thus taking up the burdens (her history of suffering) that she carries on her scarred back, which make her legs too weak to run.

Although Paul D's action might appear to smack of sexism, for he may be suggesting that Sethe is the weaker of the two of them, one would be hard-pressed to validate this view. Morrison's use of water, in the form of snow, suggests that Paul D's action is not meant to scoff condescendingly at Sethe's strength. The falling snow is fluid, rather than static like the frozen pond. It is poetic, soft like a secret, though it crashes "like nickels on stone" (129). This oxymoronic quality of the falling snow suggests the irony that we must conclude is present in yet another Morrisonian act of turning things upside down. Here, frozen water, unlike in the ice skating scene, is aqua vitae, new life. In spite of its inevitable harshness, signified by the jarring sound of nickels falling against stone, the snow also yields moments of sensitivity and pliability in its quietude. "Mercy," the recipients prayerfully whisper in reverence, and their skins do not turn to pewter in the softness of sunset (significantly, we are not told it is premature) and the drifting snow. It is of little wonder that although Beloved would literally transform the scene into coldness by suddenly appearing, and that although Sethe would continue to fear the possibility of bearing another child, Paul D's rusted heart would begin to melt into a firm heartbeat (no doubt a form of resurrection) that night as they fall asleep locked in each other's arms, with Sethe's hand resting firmly on Paul D's chest.

The second instance is perhaps the most important because it is the ultimate test of the parameter and depth of Paul D's declared love for and commitment to Sethe. Traumatized when Sethe confirms Stamp Paid's revelation of her crime, Paul D takes flight, abandoning her and seeking sanctuary in a local church, the Church of the Holy Redeemer, while taking refuge in wine. In a more detailed conversation with Stamp Paid, Paul D is ultimately sensitized to Sethe's plight and grows not only to understand better her "rough response to the Fugitive Bill" (171) but also to realize that he did not have the right to judge her. Significantly, too, he seems to realize the meaning of Sethe's conviction that "Love is or it ain't. Thin love ain't love of all" (164), by realizing that even his fear of Sethe was not justification enough to abandon her or his love for her. Coming to care more about how and why he had left, he is able to humble himself, feeling remorse for having referred to Sethe in animalistic terms.

Paul D's retreat to the church represents his continued if not desperate quest for psychological and spiritual wholeness. Finding that his effort to achieve it through Sethe had failed, he turns to a more conventional avenue, religion, even though other members of the community, as Stamp Paid assured him, would gladly have offered him shelter. It is clear, however, that he desires more than what they have to give. It is soon made evident as well that the church is ineffectual. Although Paul D finds asylum solely in the cellar, he continues to seek refuge in his warm bottle of wine: "The damp cellar was fairly warm, but there was no light lighting the pallet or the washbasin or the nail from which a man's clothes could be hung" (218).

The absence of light here and Paul D's lack of respect for the cross that rockets from the building—he is accused of desecrating it by drinking wine in front of it—indicate his inability to find redemption in the Church of the Holy Redeemer. For him, traditional Christianity, as it is practiced in his environment, does not lead to the path of spiritual and psychological self. Like Soaphead Church of *The Bluest Eye* and Shadrack of *Sula,* Paul D must reject such conventional avenues because they make the individual depend too much on the external for the realization of the self, impeding the achievement of a more authentic existence.

Thus, Morrison questions here again, as she seems to do in the other novels, the role of Christianity in the achievement of authentic existence that her major characters seek. As Grace Ann Hovet and Barbara Lounsberry argue, although the church is a "traditional ordering principle for Blacks," Morrison "seems clearly to have little faith in the

ability of the traditional institutions of human betterment to generate
support and liberation for [Blacks]."[38] This is why Baby Suggs, feeling
defeated by God, surrenders to death.

Failing to offer fulfillment and reaffirmation of self through the
existential action of the individual, the church in *Beloved* emerges as yet
another symbolic death experience in Paul D's life. That the cellar is
like his wooden grave in Alfred, Georgia, is clearly suggested by the
images of imprisonment and death present in two significant biblical
allusions. First is the allusion to the prison experience of the biblical
Paul, who was left in darkness to lie on a pallet; then there is the
allusion to the crucifixion in the nail on the wall on which Paul D
would hang his clothes and, again, in the pallet that would serve as his
bier.

Paul D's life, as the text successfully establishes with the recurring
themes of death and rebirth, is not a passive one but a continuing effort
to overcome and transcend the social, political, and economic restraints
that surround him. Thus, when the church emerges as a form of psychological bondage and spiritual impotence, it is logical that he would
seek to overcome it as well. Consequently, he leaves the darkness of his
cellar for the light on the porch and, more important, a conversation
with Stamp Paid, whose very name embodies personal affirmation and
authenticity.

During slavery and before he escaped north to freedom, Stamp Paid
faced head-on the castration build into the very fabric of slavery. Although tempted to destroy his wife and a master that had made her his
concubine, Stamp Paid resisted, transcending in the end the kind of
defeat that had driven Halle insane. He took control of his life by
aborting his slave name, Joshua, which means "Jehovah is salvation,"
and took the name "Stamp Paid," indicating his liberation and his sense
of being debt free. No one else was responsible for his salvation. More
important, he successfully converted his hatred into love, making an
offering of himself to the runaways he conveys across the Ohio River.
Stamp Paid acted to chart the direction of his own life in the significant
rite of naming and sacrificing himself for others, acted to benefit others
in sacrificing himself. He had, in short, become a truly holy redeemer.

Paul D's final conversation with this Christ-like figure paves the way
for his resurrection from his grave (cellar), renewed with an awareness
of the meaning of his own life as well as the gift of love that he, too, has
to share with humanity, beginning with Sethe. Thus, in another curious act of topsy-turvying, Morrison makes Paul D's cellar both his

grave and a nurturing womb that will serve as a vehicle for his final rebirth. Like the wooden prison and muddy grave in Georgia from which he propelled himself, the cellar, significantly described as "damp and fairly warm," functions as nest for the resurrected phoenix. His rebirth here is more significant, however, because he returns, like Christ, with the "good news" that Sethe needs to hear as she lies on her deathbed.

Finding her contemplating colors as she lies on Baby Suggs's bed at Bluestone Road, Paul D listens as Sethe tearfully laments the final departure of her baby Beloved. "She was my best thing," she tells him; he responds, "You your best thing, Sethe. You are" (273). The profundity of his utterance is sustained by the crucial ritual of cleansing that follows, for he offers to wash her feet, reminiscent of Baby Suggs's washing of Sethe when she finally arrived in Ohio.

The significant signs, sacraments, and symbols—the cross, wine, washing of feet—make Paul D a resurrected Christ who has clearly achieved a higher level of consciousness. Like Stamp Paid, he achieves a certain level of authentic existence and firm sense of wholeness. He becomes his own "holy redeemer." His sense of fulfillment comes from within, as his advice to Sethe clearly implies; for he, too, must have reached the realization that he is his own best thing before he could attempt to pass it on. Paul D is finally able to look at Sethe on more than a superficial level. Seeing her for the first time with a more authentic perspective, he comes to accept her as a friend of his mind: "She is a friend of my mind. She gather me, man. The pieces I am, she gather them and give them back to me in all the right order. It's good, you know, when you got a woman who is a friend of your mind" (272–73).

Mysticism and Magic

As she seems to have done with other categories employed in our study and discussion of *Beloved,* Morrison pulls out all stops in her use of mysticism and magic to accentuate their intricacies as well as their manifold presence in African-American culture. Their multifaceted qualities are ever present throughout the text and visible in everything from Morrison's use of folk medicine—salt and spiderweb—to supernatural and folk belief: "You know as well as I do [Ella tells Stamp Paid] people who die bad don't stay in the ground" (188). Their presence confirms if not crystallizes the fact that mysticism and magic are not only seminal in Morrison's collected works but often the centerpieces.

This is certainly the case in *Beloved,* which many of the first reviewers described as "a ghost story about history."[39] Specifically, what concerned a majority of the reviewers was the haunting presence of the otherworldly Beloved. As Paul Gray noted in his *Time* magazine review, Beloved's flesh and blood presence "roils the novel's intense, realistic surface."[40] Clearly, Morrison's desire is not, as Crouch wrote, to be a "literary conjure woman."[41] As noted earlier, however, she seems to operate from a premise that cultural affirmation is attainable through a matrix formed by mythology and folklore, not just the African-American but all mythologies and folk material. As suggested in this study and as Freiert correctly noted: "Morrison, an engrossing story-teller, draws deeply on Judeo-Christian tradition, on Germanic folktale, and classical themes."[42]

Furthermore, Morrison seems willing to question the superficial boundaries that she finds humankind has established between the physical and the spiritual worlds. Boundaries between myth and reality not only disappear in *Beloved,* as they do in *Tar Baby* and *Song of Solomon,* but, through the character of Beloved, are violated to probe their reality and, more important, to explore the possibility of the existence of various levels of consciousness. Thomas R. Edwards is correct in stating that Beloved "is no mere apparition. She is solidly physical"; she is not a "projection of a neurotic observer, or a superstitious mass of delusion."[43]

Yet, Beloved's presence should not be surprising; examples of Morrison's interest in mysticism and the supernatural are abundant. There is, for example, Soaphead Church, a spiritualist who uses magic to ostensibly grant Pecola her desired blue eyes in *The Bluest Eye.* There are Eva's dream book of numbers, her superstitions about attending a wedding in a red dress and about the flock of blackbirds that marked Sula's return to the Bottom, and Ajax's conjuring mother in *Sula.* There is the navelless shaman Pilate who keeps her dead father's bones in her house and communicates with the dead in *Song of Solomon.* And there are the visitations experienced by Valerian Street in *Tar Baby.*

Equally visible is Morrison's fascination with numbers, colors, plants, flowers, metals, and the elements, all of which are important to the worlds of numerology, alchemy, and mysticism; yet all would also be considered natural and useful symbols and tropes to a writer of Morrison's caliber. Morrison almost always selects numbers that are ascribed with magical powers; for example, one, three, seven, and 22, which are associated with completion and creation. Her successful communities of women are almost always triadic. Important addresses have the base number of seven, such as "7 Carpenter's Road" and "124 Blue-stone Road," whose numbers total seven, the number of creation. Drawing from astronomy, Morrison provides a lunar cycle, 28 days of happiness, as a trope for Sethe's freedom. Numerologically speaking this number's total is one (2 + 8 = 10; 1 + 0 = 1), a symbol of wholeness and completion; but it is also four times seven, suggestive of the cycles of completeness and renewal. She also draws upon the notion that colors have symbolic powers and characteristics of their own. Red and yellow and their combination, orange, are complexly used. There is, for example, the power of the woman in yellow in *Tar Baby*, who leaves gold tracks on the floor. There is the orange square in the quilt that Baby Suggs contemplates before dying. There is the red of Beloved's blood, the blood on the rose Paul D sees on the way to the carnival, and the fire red of Six-O's tongue. Colors are often juxtaposed with metal, such as gold with yellow (mentioned above), the iron bit that Paul D licks with his red tongue, and the pewter of the women's skin on the frozen pond. Morrison offers no uniformity or unity in her use of these fundamental symbols and tropes found in all literatures; in fact, she varies their meaning in her text from time to time. Red may sometimes be associated with passion, but it may also be associated with oppression.

Morrison's tendency to shatter conventional meanings and interpretations as she draws on more conventional myths and folk material is most visible in her use of Sethe's name, which she obviously borrows from the Seth who was one of the major gods of ancient Egypt and the biblical Seth who was the child of Adam and Eve and whose descendants include Noah and his grandson Ham, who was cursed for having seen his grandfather naked. This biblical mythology was often used to justify the enslavement/oppression of blacks. It is the irony that we face when we consider the physical appearance of the Egyptian mythical Seth that is important to Morrison's use of the name. In form he was part man and part animal or bird (perhaps a falcon); he was often connected with purification rituals.

Interestingly enough, what remains problematic for Morrison's Sethe is schoolteacher's concentration on her more "animalistic" characteristics in his effort to denigrate her and the other Sweet Home slaves. Yet, in reporting her action at the time she attempts to protect her children, Morrison's narrator describes Sethe's behavior with birdlike images: Sethe "heard wings. Little hummingbirds stuck their needle beaks right through her headcloth into her hair and beat their wings . . . She just flew" (163). Also, when she thinks the grown Beloved is in danger, "She hears wings. Little hummingbirds stick needle beaks right through her headcloth into her hair and beat their wings . . . She flies" (262).

Sethe's indirect association with cows draws fully on the ancient mythologies and religion that her name suggests. We are told that while waiting for Sethe's arrival, the Sweet Home men wasted themselves on cows. After witnessing Halle's and Sethe's first sexual experience, Paul D thinks, "The jump . . . from a calf to a girl wasn't all that mighty" (26). Paul D would direct his most wounding remark at Sethe with images that presumably associate her with a cow: "You got two feet, Sethe, not four" (165).

Viewed strictly in the physionomystic realm of schoolteacher and the chattel world of economic slavery, the association of Sethe with an animal is at best insulting and at worst degrading, but viewed in the mythical and mystical world of ancient Egypt (again perhaps the origin of Sethe's name), one may come to envision a goddess such as Hathor, mother of the sun god, who had a human face but the ears and horns of a cow. In mythology, moreover, a cow is generally seen as the giver of life. Because of its fecundity, the cow, like the earth, is often mother goddess, nurturer, and provider of food (milk), a life giving source (in Hinduism for example). Thus, by topsy-turvying the traditional negative stereotypes of chattel slavery, Morrison successfully elevates Sethe to the level of goddess through her selection of name alone.

Morrison's propensity to explore myths, mysticism, and magic—can be clearly seen from the above assessment. Her propensity to create, revise, and rewrite her own provide clear insight into her use of Beloved as character. Sethe's slain daughter does indeed allow us to probe any superficial boundaries between myth and reality, as Morrison might perceive them. More important, however, through her use of Beloved we find Morrison reaching deep into African-American oral folk culture not only to utilize one of the gems that lie at the very foundation of the more formal (written) African-American literary tradition but to demonstrate her talents as a master story teller.

That Morrison draws upon a folk motif that is familiar to African-American culture is supported by some of the tales Richard M. Dorson included under "Spirits and Haunts" in his *American Negro Folktales.* That she draws as well on traditional African folklore and practices may be validated by John S. Mbiti's discussion of "Spiritual Beings, Spirit and Living-dead" in his *African Religions and Philosophies.* Mbiti informs us that traditional African philosophy "emphasized that the spiritual universe is a unit with the physical, and that these two intermingle and dovetail into each other so much that it is not easy, or even necessary, at times to draw the distinctions or separate them."[44]

In the end, Morrison's success in this novel must be viewed in relation to her use of the oral tradition of folk art in general, which would necessarily include the mystical. Here spontaneity and newness are key elements, for they contribute to the ultimate goal of the story teller: to create a tale in which the process of telling the story is just as important as the tale itself. This is what is known by one of Dorson's collaborators, a master story teller who, incidentally, is named Suggs. Dorson writes, "Unquenchable, fraternal, Suggs still wore the badge of the minstrel entertainer, breaking into story, jest, song, and even dance when the spotlight swung his way . . . But in another mood he turned crackerbox philosopher, and moralized on human behavior in simple Biblical terms . . . The candor of his conversational sallies left me agape."[45] Dorson also wrote that Suggs and the other collaborators "believed in hoodoo, spirits, and the literal word of the Bible, whose store of marvels they continually cited to underpin their own wondrous tales."[46]

In *Beloved* Morrison becomes the engrossing story teller that Freiert claims she is, but she goes beyond that to show as well that she is a grand mistress of the oral tradition, leading us to believe that at the site of memory she found the remnants of others like her.

Chapter Seven
Pass It On

It seems appropriate to end this excursion into the world of Toni Morrison as we began it, by having her speak for herself. In 1977, in an interview with radio talk show host Steve Cannon and dramatist/poet Ntozake Shange, Morrison offered a candid insight into her goal as a writer. Near the end of the interview, Cannon asked her to elaborate on what, in the final analysis, she was attempting to do in her novels, and specifically in *Song of Solomon,* which had recently been published. Morrison's response is significant enough to quote in its entirety:

My attempt, although I never say any of this, until I'm done . . . is to deal with something that is nagging me, but, when I think about it in a large sense, I use the phrase "bear witness" to explain what my work is for. I have this creepy sensation . . . of loss. Like something is either lost, never to be retrieved, or something is about to be lost and will never be retrieved. Because if *we* don't know it (what our past is), if we women don't know it, then nobody in the world knows it—nobody in our civilization knows it. . . . But if we women, if we black women, if we Third-World women in America don't know it, then, it is not known by anybody at all. And I mean that. Then nobody knows it. And somebody has to tell somebody something.[1]

Without a doubt, as noted earlier, Morrison refers here to the act of rememory, of tapping into the deepest recesses of consciousness, of ripping the veil so that one's interior life and history can surface. For black women, in particular (and they are obviously an important part of Morrison's audience), this is crucial; it gives them access once again to what Alice Walker called their "mother's garden," a fertile soil for growth and development.

Her comments are not limited to black women, however; our examination in this text supports the belief that Morrison's effort throughout her literary career has been to "tell somebody something," something that has been lost and forgotten, stories that have not been passed on. At the end of *Beloved,* Morrison seems to ask the reader to pass the stories on, to stand, as does Morrison, and bear witness to them. Thus, the question must be asked, What is it that Morrison feels has been omitted, lost, or forgotten? What must be unearthed and passed on? Finally, To whom and for whom must this all be done?

As pointed out in chapter 6, Morrison makes it all very clear in her remarks in "Site of Memory." Ripping the veil that obscures the truth, particularly about black Americans, stands at the top of her list. Morrison dedicated *Beloved* to the sixty million or more black Africans who were brought to the New World as slaves, and she confesses that she was interested in showing the malevolence of slavery. Once ripped, the veil of segregation and oppression reveals the historical, psychological, spiritual, and physical damages of slavery. As she does so, the author bears witness to its horror.

Thus, Morrison writes to and for blacks. She has no problems stating this fact. "When I view the world, perceive it and write it, it is the world of black people. It is not that I won't write about white people. I just know that when I'm trying to develop the various themes I write about, the people who best manifest these for me are the black people whom I invent. It is not deliberate or calculated or self-consciously black, because I recognize and despise the artificial black writing some writers do."[2] As Morrison told Walter Clemons, however, this does not mean that whites cannot adequately respond to her works. "When I write, I don't try to translate for white readers . . . Dostoevski wrote for a Russian audience, but we're able to read him. If I'm specific, and I don't overexplain, then anybody can overhear me."[3]

It is clear, then, that Morrison sees her work as speaking to a specific audience but as reaching beyond the bounds of that audience to the rest of humankind. As we suggested above, Morrison uses the black slave experience in America as a metaphor for the human condition, which is necessarily all-inclusive.

What seems equally horrific for Morrison, in the long run, what seems to nag at her is the apparent loss of compound, of village, of community, of neighborhood (a significant trope in her texts) that she sees. Although it is specifically a black community, it is inevitably the larger community of humankind as well. The global family is out of sync. Morrison explains that "family" is whatever the neighborhood is, but that the neighborhood does not have to be one street: "It could be two people in California, one in Georgia, one in Maine . . ."[4] In today's world of materialism, Morrison maintains, it is infinitely easier to be an individual than to be a community. This is one of the themes of *Tar Baby*. What must be remembered, borne witness to, and passed on is the value of community—of the human community.

In Morrison's fictional world, however, *neighborhood* is not synony-mous with *encroachment*. Thus, concomitantly, the salience of authentic existence is witnessed and passed on. But an authentic existence, in the final analysis, is not grounded in a mere sense of "me-ness," although it does encourage the individual to protect him- or herself against forces that destroy the significance of the self, forces that bombard and frag-ment interior life. The authentic individual in Morrison's world realizes that his or her rights, duties, and responsibilities in the neighborhood of humankind are to act, to choose. The individual must realize the absolute freedom to choose. As Morrison told Gloria Naylor, "The point is that freedom is choosing your responsibility. It's not having no responsibilities, it's choosing the ones you want."[5]

We have demonstrated in this discussion that Morrison's protago-nists who express either the "effort of will" or a "freedom of will" live richer, more meaningful lives, although their lives might be said to be dangerously free. The danger emerges from the nature of what is an existential perspective, for it is a freedom that is not without responsi-bility, the responsibility for the neighborhood, and thus one that might involve angst. Although Morrison's characters who act existentially do so by assuming full responsibility for their lives, their existences, we noted, are ones in which they are responsible for both the self *and* the world as a way of being. It seems perfectly all right for Sula to be me-centered, but she committed an unpardonable crime when she put Eva in the rest home.

Sartre and Morrison seem to agree that "Man is nothing but what he makes of himself," but that in his freedom he "carries the weight of the world on his shoulders."[6] Guitar of *Song of Solomon* (in spite of his membership in a vigilante group) seems to echo Sartre when he tells Milkman: "It is not about you living longer. Its about how you live and why" (161). Morrison amplifies this basic premise by adding the signifi-cance of a "willingness to love" one's fellowman to her formula (*Song of Solomon*, 226). Pilate, one of Morrison's most humane characters, ex-claims upon her death: "I wish I'd a known more people. I would of loved 'em all. If I'd a knowed more, I would a loved more" (*Song of Solomon*, 340). Ultimately, what remains of paramount importance to Morrison is the salience of human worth. This above all must be witnessed and passed on. One of the inevitable results of Morrison's tendency to exaggerate, a seminal aspect of her style, is that readers are forced to think about the latter, recall it, and maybe be concerned enough to pass it on.

As a result of her literary and artistic abilities and competence, Toni Morrison stands in the vanguard of contemporary writers of fiction. We must note, however, that her success as a writer transcends both her racial identity and gender. She is not only a leading African-American woman novelist, though this is most noteworthy, she is one of the most significant and relevant writers on the literary scene today. Her acclaim is international; her novels are translated into many languages. Scholars and doctoral candidates the world over critique and assess her works, seeking to unravel the complexity that Morrison prides. She confesses, "It is the complexity and subtlety in [the work] that is interesting to me more than the little plot."[7]

An astute scholar as well as a uniquely creative writer, Morrison has won the deepest respect and admiration of both her fellow writers and the populace at large. In addition to the feature coverage she has received from the popular media, from major national magazines and journals, she has been the recipient of several honorary degrees, literary awards, and domestic recognitions. Her place in American letters leaves her standing next to such eminent writers as Henry David Thoreau, Sherwood Anderson, Sinclair Lewis, and William Faulkner. She ranks worldwide with the masters Dostoevsky and Gabriel Garcia Marquez. Like these writers, Morrison's ultimate message is that each person should and must respect the reality of the human landscape of the world, with its unlimited possibilities and interpretations, if humankind is to achieve wholeness, if the global community is to once again be whole. Pass it on.

Notes and References

Preface

1. Toni Morrison, "Behind the Making of *The Black Book,*" *Black World* 23(1974):xxx.
2. Frances Taliaferro, "Books in Brief," *Harper's Magazine,* January 1978, 94.
3. Thomas R. Edward, "Ghost Story," *New York Review of Books,* 5 November 1987, 19.
4. Claudia Tate, "Toni Morrison" in *Black Women Writers at Work* ed. Claudia Tate (New York: Continuum, 1983), 120.
5. Jean Strouse, "Toni Morrison: Black Magic," *Newsweek,* 30 March 1981, 52.
6. Diana Johnson, "The Oppressor in the Next Room," *The New York Review,* 10 November 1977, 6.
7. Tate, "Toni Morrison," 125.
8. Ntozake Shange, "Interview with Toni Morrison." *American Rag,* November 1978, 48.
9. Leslie B. Washington, "Toni Morrison Now," *Essence,* October 1987, 137.
10. Walter Clemons, "A Gravestone of Memories," *Newsweek,* 28 September 1987, 75.

Chapter One

1. Clenora Hudson-Weems and Wilfred D. Samuels, interview with Toni Morrison, New York, 17 June 1985 (unpublished).
2. Ibid.
3. Toni Morrison, "Behind the Making of *The Black Book,*" *Black World* 23 (1974):90.
4. *The Bluest Eye* (New York: Washington Square Press, 1970). Page references in text.
5. See interview with Colette Dowling, *New York Times Magazine,* 20 May 1979, 42.
6. Strouse, "Toni Morrison," 53.
7. Carolyn F. Gerald, "The Black Writer and His Role," in *The Black Aesthetics,* ed. Addison Gayle, Jr. (New York: Anchor Books, 1970), 349–56.
8. Toni Morrison, "Slow Walk of Trees . . ." *New York Times Magazine,* 4 July 1976, 152.

9. Strouse, "Toni Morrison," 54.
10. Colette Dowling, "The Song of Toni Morrison," *New York Times Magazine*, 20 May 1971, 42.
11. Morrison, "Slow Walk," 150.
12. Morrison, "Behind the Making," 88.
13. Robert Stepto, "Intimate Things in Place: A Conversation with Toni Morrison," in *Chant of Saints*, ed. Michael S. Harper and Robert Stepto (Urbana: University of Illinois Press, 1979), 214.
14. Strouse, "Toni Morrison," 54.
15. Morrison keeps her family life very private; she doesn't care to engage in public discussions about her exhusband or her two sons.
16. John Leonard, review in *New York Times Book Review*, 1 November 1970, 9.
17. Mel Watkins, "Talk with Toni Morrison," *New York Times Book Review* 11 September 1977, 50.
18. Thomas LeClair, " 'The Language Must Not Sweat,' A Conversation with Toni Morrison," *New Republic*, 21 March 1981, 25.
19. Hudson-Weems and Samuels, interview.
20. Sara Blackburn, review in *New York Book Review*, 30 December 1973, 3.
21. Morrison, "Behind the Making."
22. *Nation*, 19 November 1977, 536.
23. Reynolds Price, review in *New York Times Book Review*, 11 September 1977, 1.
24. Strouse, "Toni Morrison," 52.
25. Al Silverman, "A Talk With Toni Morrison," *Book of the Month Club Newsletter* (Fall 1987):5.
26. Ibid.
27. Walter Clemons, "A Gravestone of Memories," *Newsweek*, 28 September 1987, 75.
28. Wilfrid Sheed, "*Beloved* by Toni Morrison," *Book of the Month Club Newsletter* (Fall 1987).

Chapter Two

1. Gerald, "The Black Writer," 352, 349–56.
2. Morrison, "Behind the Making," 89.
3. Philip Royster, "The Bluest Eye," *First World* (1977):38.
4. Toni Morrison, letter to students at Head Royce School, Oakland, California, 30 June 1980 (unpublished).
5. Royster, "Bluest Eye," 35.
6. Cynthia A. Davis, "Self, Society, and Myth in Toni Morrison's Fiction," *Contemporary Literature* 23(1982):330.
7. Houston A. Baker, Jr., *Blues, Ideology and Afro-American Literature: A Vernacular Theory* (Chicago: The University of Chicago Press, 1984), 147.

8. Jean Paul Sartre, *Being and Nothingness,* trans. Hazel E. Barnes (New York: Washington Square Press, 1966), 52.

9. Ibid., 317–19, 310–35.

10. Robert Denoon Cumming, ed., *The Philosophy of Jean-Paul Sartre* (New York: Vintage Books, 1965), 196.

11. Hazel E. Barnes, *The Meddling Gods* (Lincoln: University of Nebraska Press, 1974), 23.

12. Keith Byerman, *Fingering the Jagged Grain, Tradition and Form in Recent Black Fiction* (Athens: University of Georgia Press, 1985), 189–90.

13. Ibid., 189.

14. Chiwenye Okonjo Oguyemi, "Order and Disorder in Toni Morrison's *The Bluest Eye,*" *Critique: Studies in Modern Fiction* 19(1977):119.

15. Gloria Wade-Gayles, *No Crystal Stair* (New York: Pilgrim Press, 1984), 143.

16. Ibid., 144.

17. Davis, "Self, Society, and Myth," 333.

18. Byerman, *Fingering the Jagged Grain,* 191–92.

19. The distinctions between external and internal narration made by Genette seem applicable to this novel. See Gerard Genette, *Narrative Discourse, An Essay in Method,* trans. Jane E. Lewis (Ithaca: Cornell University Press, 1980), 186–94.

20. Phyllis R. Klotman, "Dick-and-Jane and the Shirley Temple Sensibility in *The Bluest Eye,*" *Black American Literature Forum* 13(1979):124.

21. Barbara Christian, "Community and Nature: The Novels of Toni Morrison," *The Journal of Ethnic Studies* 7 (1980):66.

22. Klotman, "Dick-and-Jane," 124.

23. Trudier Harris, *From Mammies to Militants, Domestics in Black American Literature* (Philadelphia: Temple University Press, 1982), 59–69.

24. Wade-Gayles, *No Crystal Stair,* 141.

25. Calvin Hernton, *The Sexual Mountain and Black Women Writers* (New York: Doubleday, Anchor Press, 1987), 11, 17.

26. Jacqueline de Weever, "The Inverted World of Toni Morrison's *The Bluest Eye* and *Sula,*" *CLA Journal,* 22, (June 1979):403.

27. Herton, *The Sexual Mountain,* 18.

28. Davis, "Self, Society, and Myth," 227.

29. W. Lawrence Hogue, *Discourse and the Other* (Durham: Duke University Press, 1986), 133.

Chapter Three

1. Tate, "Toni Morrison," 125.

2. Naama Banyiwa-Horne, "The Scary Face of the Self: An Analysis of the Character Sula in Toni Morrison's *Sula,*" *Sage* 2(1985):28.

3. *Sula* (New York: Bantam Books, 1975). Page references in text.

4. Pearl K. Bell, "Self Seekers," *Commentary* 72(1981):56.

5. Odette A. Martin, "Sula," *First World* 1(1977):41.

6. Stepto, "Intimate Things," 214.

7. Addison Gayle, "Blueprint for Black Criticism," *First World* 1(1977):44.

8. Susan Willis, *Specifying, Black Women Writing, The American Experience* (Madison: The University of Wisconsin Press, 1987), 94.

9. Ibid.

10. Philip Royster, "A Spider and a Snake," *Umoja* 2(1978):164.

11. Banyiwa-Horne, "The Scary Face," 31.

12. Stepto, "Intimate Things," 216–17.

13. Tate, "Toni Morrison," 129.

14. Martin, "Sula," 36.

15. Grace Ann Hovet and Barbara Lounsberry, "Principles of Perception in Toni Morrison's *Sula*," *Black American Literature Forum* 13(1979):126.

16. Martin, "Sula," 43.

17. Chiwenye Okonjo Ogunyemi, "*Sula:* 'A Nigger Joke,' " *Black American Literature Forum* 13 (1979):133.

18. Martin, "Sula," 41.

19. Cynthia Dubin Edelberg, "Morrison's Voice: Formal Education, The Work Ethics, and the Bible," *American Literature* 58 (1986):226.

20. Ibid., 219, 223.

21. Ibid., 223.

22. Erich Neumann, *The Great Mother*, trans. Ralph Manheim (Princeton: Princeton University Press, 1972), 18–23; 147–50.

23. John Mbiti, *African Religions and Philosophies* (New York: Anchor, 1970), 102–18.

24. Christian, "Community and Nature," 54.

25. Byerman, *Fingering the Jagged Grain*, 198.

26. Tate, "Toni Morrison," 118.

27. Betty J. Parker, "Complexity: Toni Morrison's Women—An Interview Essay," in *Sturdy Black Bridges*, ed. Rosean P. Bell et al. (New York: Anchor Books, 1979), 253.

28. Hovet and Lounsberry, "Principles of Perception," 128.

29. Violet S. deLaszlo, ed., *The Basic Writings of C. G. Jung* (New York: Modern Library, 1959), 144.

30. Ogunyemi, "*Sula*," 132.

31. deLaszlo, *Basic Writings of C. G. Jung*, 55.

32. Ibid., 112.

33. Tate, "Toni Morrison," 125.

Chapter Four

1. Tate, "Toni Morrison," 125.

2. Grace A. Hovet and Barbara Lounsberry, "Flying as Symbol and Legend," CLA Journal XXVII 2 (1983):136.

3. Mel Watkins, "Talk."

4. *Song of Solomon* (New York: New American Library, 1977). Page references in text.

5. Hudson-Weems and Samuels, interview.

6. Shange, "Interview," 50.

7. Ibid., 49.

8. William K. Freiert, "Classical Themes in *Song of Solomon, Helios* 10 (1983):165.

9. Hovet and Lounsberry, "Flying," 137.

10. Anne Mickelson, *Reaching Out* (Metachen, New Jersey: Scarecrow Press, 1979), 173.

11. Christian, "Community and Nature," 72

12. Susan L. Blake, "Folklore and Community in *Song of Solomon,*" *Melus* 7 (1980):78.

13. Arnold Van Gennep, *The Rites of Passage* (Chicago: University of Chicago Press, 1978):1–13.

14. Victor Turner, *The Forest of Symbols* (Ithaca: Cornell University Press, 1967):93–111. Also "Myth and Symbols," *Encyclopedia of Social Sciences,* 10(1968):576–81.

15. Freiert, "Classical Themes," 161–70. Also Wilfred D. Samuels, "Liminality and the Search for Self in Toni Morrison's *Song of Solomon,*" *Minority Voices* 5(1981):59–68.

16. Samuels, "Liminality," 64.

17. Turner, "Myth and Symbols," 577.

18. Phillip Royster, "Milkman's Flying: The Scapegoat Transcended in Toni Morrison's *Song of Solomon,*" *CLA Journal* 23(1982):438.

19. Susan Willis, "Eruptions of Funk: Historicizing Toni Morrison," *Black American Literature Forum* 16(1982):37.

20. Bonnie Bartold, *Black Time,* 176.

21. Blake, "Folklore," 79.

22. Ibid., 80.

23. Shange, "Interview," 48.

24. Shange, "Interview," 48–49.

25. Hudson-Weems and Samuels, interview.

26. Leslie Harris, "Myth as Structure in Toni Morrison's *Song of Solomon,*" *Meleus* 7(Fall 1980):70.

27. Chiara Spallino, "*Song of Solomon:* An Adventure in Structure," CALLALOO 8(1985), 510.

28. Shange, "Interview," 48.

29. Dorothy H. Lee, "*Song of Solomon:* To Ride the Air," *Black American Literature Forum,* 16 (1982):70.

Chapter Five

1. James Coleman, "The Quest for Wholeness in Toni Morrison's *Tar Baby*," *Black American Literature Forum* 20(1986), 66.
2. *Tar Baby* (New York: Knopf, 1981). Page references in text.
3. Barbara Christian, "Trajectories of Self-Definition: Placing Contemporary Afro-American Women's Fiction," in *Conjuring: Black Women, Fiction, and Literary Tradition,* ed. Marjorie Pryse and Hortense J. Spillers (Bloomington: Indiana University Press, 1985), 244.
4. Angelita Reyes, "Ancient Properties in the New World: The Paradox of the 'Other' in Toni Morrison's *Tar Baby*," *Black Scholar* 17 (March 1986):19.
5. See Reyes's definition of this term in "Ancient Properties," 20.
6. Reyes, "Ancient Properties," 23.
7. Coleman, "The Quest," 68.
8. Bartold, *Black Time,* passim.
9. Coleman, "The Quest," 65.
10. Strouse, "Toni Morrison," 57.
11. Josie P. Campbell, "To Sing the Song, To Tell the Tale: A Study of Toni Morrison and Simone Schwarz-Bart," *Comparative Literature Studies* 20, no. 3 (Fall 1985):402.
12. Hudson-Weems and Samuels, interview.
13. Terry Otten, "The Crime of Innocence in Toni Morrison's *Tar Baby*," *Studies in American Fiction* (Autumn 1986,) 14, no. 2:161.
14. Edelberg, "Morrison's Voice," 232.
15. Christian, "Trajectories," 243.
16. Edelberg, "Morrison's Voice," 235.
17. Wade-Gayles, *No Crystal Stair,* 220.
18. Hudson-Weems and Samuels, interview.
19. Ibid.
20. Campbell, "To Sing," 409.

Chapter Six

1. These writers and critics submitted a letter to the *New York Times Book Review,* which read in part: "The legitimate need for our own critical voice in relation to our own literature can no longer be denied. We, therefore, urgently affirm our rightful and positive authority in the realm of American letters and, in this prideful context, we do raise this tribute to the author of *The Bluest Eye, Sula, Song of Solomon, Tar Baby,* and *Beloved.* See *New York Times,* 24 January 1988, 36.
2. *Beloved* (New York: Knopf, 1987). Page references in text.
3. Toni Morrison, "The Site of Memory," in *Inventing the Truth, The Art and Craft of Memoir,* ed. William Zinsser (Boston: Houghton Mifflin, 1987), 119.

4. Bill Cosby, "Introduction," in *The Black Book,* comp. Middleton Harris (New York: Random House, 1973), i.

5. Marsha Darling, "In the Realm of Responsibility, A Conversation with Toni Morrison," *The Women's Review of Books* 5 (March 1988):5.

6. Ibid.

7. Frances Smith Foster, *Witnessing Slavery, The Development of Antebellum Slave Narratives* (Westport, Connecticut: Greenwood Press, 1979), 3.

8. Ibid., 84.

9. Ibid., 13.

10. Ibid., 13–14.

11. Morrison, "Site," 109.

12. Barbara Christian, "From the Inside Out," *CHS Occasional Papers* 19 (Univeristy of Minnesota Press, 1987), 9.

13. Morrison, "Site," 113, 11?.

14. Ibid., 113.

15. Frederick Douglass, *Narrative of the Life of Frederick Douglass, An American Slave* (New York: New American Library, 1968), 24–25.

16. Harriet Jacobs (Linda Brent), *Incidents in the Life of a Slave Girl,* ed. L. Maria Child (San Diego: Harvest Books, 1973), xiii.

17. Ibid., xii.

18. Christian, "From the Inside Out," 9.

19. John Hope Franklin, *From Slavery to Freedom* (New York: Knopf, 1967), 259.

20. Deborah Gray White, *Ar'n't I a Woman? Female Slaves in the Plantation South* (New York: W. W. Norton & Co. 1985), 70.

21. Ibid.

22. Nancy Chodorow, *The Reproduction of Mothering, Psychoanalysis and the Sociology of Gender* (Berkeley: University of California Press, 1978), 58–59.

23. Chodorow, *Reproduction,* 59.

24. Ibid.

25. W. E. B. DuBois, *The Souls of Black Folk* (Greenwich, Conn: Fawcett Publications, 1961), 152–56.

26. Michael Balint, *Primary Love and Psycho-Analytic Technique* (New York: Liverlight Publishing Corporation, 1953), 119.

27. White, *Ar'n't I a Woman?,* 76–77.

28. Ibid., 77.

29. Ibid., 88.

30. Balint, *Primary Love,* 120.

31. Ibid., 119.

32. See Edward Morgolies *The Art of Richard Wright* (Carbondale: Southern Illinois Press, 1969):122.

33. Interview with Charlene Hunter Gault, "MacNeil/Lehrer News & World Report."

34. Stanley Crouch, "Aunt Medea," *New Republic,* 19 October 1987, 40.

35. White, *Ar'n't I a Woman?,* 119.

36. Ibid., 121.

37. Robert Stepto, *From Behind the Veil, A Study of Afro-American Narrative* (Urbana: University of Illinois Press, 1979), 68.

38. Hovet and Lounsberry, "Principles and Perception," 128.

39. See John Leonard's review of *Beloved* for the *L.A. Times Book Review,* 30 August 1987, 1.

40. Paul Gray, "Something Terrible Happened," *Time,* 21 September 1987, 75.

41. Crouch, "Aunt Medea," 40.

42. Freiert, "Classical Themes," 161. Helios 10(1983)161

43. Thomas R. Edwards, review in *New York Times Book Review,* 5 November 1987, 18.

44. Mbiti, *African Religions,* 97.

45. Dorson, *American Negro Folktales,* 24.

46. Ibid.

Chapter Seven

1. Shange, "Interview," 52.

2. Tate, "Toni Morrison," 118.

3. Walter Clemons, "The Ghost of 'Sixty Million and More,' " *Newsweek,* 28 September 1987, 75.

4. Hudson-Weems and Samuels, interview.

5. Gloria Naylor and Toni Morrison, "A Conversation," *Southern Quarterly* 21(1985):573.

6. Jean-Paul Sartre, *Existentialism and Human Emotions* (Secaucus, N.J.: Castle, n.d.):15, 52.

7. Hudson-Weems and Samuels, interview.

Selected Bibliography

PRIMARY SOURCES

Novels:

Beloved. New York: Knopf, 1987.
The Bluest Eye. New York: Holt, Rinehart, & Winston, 1970.
Song of Solomon. New York: Knopf, 1977.
Sula. New York: Knopf, 1973.
Tar Baby. New York: Knopf, 1981.

Nonfiction

"A Knowing So Deep." *Essence,* May 1985, 230.
The Black Book, compiled by Middleton Harris, edited by Toni Morrison. New York: Random House, 1974.
"Behind the Making of *The Black Book.*" *Black World* 23(1974):86–90.
"I Will Always be a Writer." *Essence,* December 1976, 54–56, 90.
"Reading." *Mademoiselle,* May 1975, 14.
"Rediscovering Black History." *New York Times Magazine,* 11 August 1974, 14, 16, 18, 20, 22, 24.
"The Site of Memory." In *Inventing the Truth, The Art and Craft of Memoir,* edited by William Zinsser. Boston: Houghton Mifflin, 1987, 103–24.
"A Slow Walk of a Tree (as Grandmother Would Say), Hopeless (as Grandfather Would Say)." *New York Times Magazine,* 4 July 1976, 104, 150, 142, 160, 162, 164.

Interviews

Bakerman, Jane. "The Seams Can't Show: An Interview with Toni Morrison." *Black American Literature Forum* 12 (1978):556–60.
Darling, Marsha. "In the Realm of Responsibility: A Conversation with Toni Morrison." *Women's Review of Books* 5 (March 1988):5–6.
Hudson-Weems, Clenora, and Wilfred D. Samuels. "An Interview with Toni Morrison." 17 June 1985. Unpublished.
LeClair, Thomas. "The Language Must Not Sweat." *New Republic,* 21 March 1981, 25–29.
Naylor, Gloria. "A Conversation, Gloria Naylor and Toni Morrison." *Southern Review* 21(1985):567–593.

Parker, Betty J. "Complexity: Toni Morrison's Women—An Interview Essay."
    In *Sturdy Black Bridges: Visions of Black Women in Literature,* edited by
    Roseann Pope Bell et al. Garden City: Doubleday, 1979, 251–57.
Shange, Ntozake. "Interview with Toni Morrison." *American Rag,* November
    1978, 48–52.
Stepto, Robert B. " 'Intimate Things in Place': A Conversation with Toni
    Morrison." *Massachusetts Review* 18 (1977):473–89. Also in *Chant of
    Saints,* edited by Robert Stepto and Michael Harper. Urbana: University
    of Illinois Press, 1979, 213–29.
Tate, Claudia. "A Conversation with Toni Morrison." In *Black Women Writers
    at Work.* New York: Continuum, 1983, 117–31.
Washington, Elsie B. "Toni Morrison Now." *Essence,* October 1987, 58, 136–
    37.
Watkins, Mel. "Talk with Toni Morrison." *New York Times Book Review,* 11
    September 1977, 48, 50.
Wilson, Judith. "Conversations with Toni Morrison." *Essence* 12 (July
    1981):84, 86, 128, 130, 133, 134.

SECONDARY SOURCES

Bibliography:

Middleton, David L. *Toni Morrison: An Annotated Bibliography.* New York:
    Garland, 1987.

Books:

Halloway, Karla F. C., and Stephanie Demetrakopoulous. *New Dimensions of
    Spirituality: A Biracial, Bicultural Reading of the Novels by Toni Morrison.*
    Greenwood, Conn.: Greenwood Press, 1987.
Jones, Bessie W., and Audrey L. Vinson. *The World of Toni Morrison: Explora-
    tions in Literary Criticism.* Dubuque, Iowa: Kendall/Hunt, 1983.
McKay, Nellie, ed., *Critical Essays on Toni Morrison.* Boston: G. K. Hall,
    1988. Collection of new essays on Morrison's first four novels.
Stepto, Robert. *From Behind the Veil, A Study of Afro-American Narrative.*
    Urbana: University of Illinois Press, 1979.

Parts of Books and Articles:

Bakerman, Jane S. "Failures of Love, Female Initiations in the Novels of Toni
    Morrison." *American Literature* 52 (1981):541–63. Examines Morrison's
    major characters' search for familial roots and personal identity through
    love.

Banyiwa-Horne, Naama. "The Scary Face of the Self: An Analysis of the Character of Sula." *Sage* 2 (1985):28–31. Explores and explains Sula's darker side by discussing her alter ego.

Barksdale, Richard K. "Castration Symbolism in Recent Black American Fiction." *College Language Association Journal* 24 (1986):400–413. A critical assessment of the treatment of black men in the works of four black women novelists, including *Sula*.

Bell, Pearl. "Self Seekers." *Commentary* 72 (1981):56–60. Weak generalizations and estimation of the individuation of the main characters in *Tar Baby*.

Blake, Susan L. "Toni Morrison." *Afro-American Fiction Writers After 1955. Dictionary of Literary Biography*, edited by Thadious M. Davis and Trudier Harris. Detroit: Gale Research Company, 1984, 187–99. General summary of works and brief biographical information.

———. "Folklore and Community in *Song of Solomon*." *Melus* 7 (1980):71–82. Discussion of the search for wholeness through myths.

Bischoff, Joan. "Studies in Thwarted Sensibility." *Studies in Black Literature* 6 (1975):21–23. A study of the frustrations and alternatives of the artist who lacks form.

Bruck, Peter. "Returning to One's Roots: The Motif of Searching and Flying in Toni Morrison's *Song of Solomon*." *The Afro-American Novel Since 1960.* Discussion of Afro-American folklore, with an examination of African heritage as genealogical guide.

Byerman, Keith. "Intense Behaviours: The Use of the Grotesque in *The Bluest Eye*, and *Eva's Man*." *College Language Association Journal* 25 (1982):447–57. Discusses Morrison's use of the grotesque as a vehicle for social criticism.

Campbell, Josie P. "To Sing the Song, To Tell the Tale: A Study of Toni Morrison and Simone Schwarz-Bart." *Comparative Literature Studies* 20 (1985):394–412. Discusses the themes of quest for self-hood and flight in *Song of Solomon* and *Tar Baby*.

Capland, Brina. "A Fierce Conflict of Colors." *Nation,* 2 May 1981, 529–35.

Christian, Barbara. "Community and Nature: The Novels of Toni Morrison." *Journal of Ethnic Studies* 7 (1980):65–78. Examines the central place of the communities of Morrison's first three novels.

———. "The Concept of Class in the Novels of Toni Morrison." *Black Feminist Criticism,* 71–80. New York: Pergamon Press, 1985. Discusses Morrison's women in relation to class and class assumptions.

———. "The Contemporary Fables of Toni Morrison." *Black Women Novelists,* edited by Barbara Christian, Westport, Connecticut: Greenwood Press, 1980, 137, 111–79. Explores the dynamics of Morrison's characters in *The Bluest Eyes* and *Sula* as they interact in a society that is caught between the tensions of the two distinct cultures, the black and the white.

———. "From the Inside Out: Afro-American Women Literary Tradition and the State." *Center for Humanistic Studies Occasional Papers.* University of Minnesota Press, 1986. Discussion of Afro-American women writers and their effort to reclaim the history passed through the memory of their mothers.

———. "Pass It On." *Black Women Novelists,* edited by Barbara Christian. Westport, Connecticut: Greenwood Press, 1980, 239–52. Discusses Morrison's development of her female characters' relationships to community, men, white society, and one another in *The Bluest Eye* and *Sula.*

———. "Trajectories of Self-Definition: Placing Contemporary Afro-American Women's Fiction." *Black Feminist Criticism: Perspectives of Black Women Writers,* 171–86. New York: Pergamon Press, 1985. Discusses problems faced by Afro-American women writers relative to a commitment to self-understanding and self-affirmation.

Coleman, James. "The Quest for Wholeness in Morrison's *Tar Baby.*" *Black American Literature Forum* 20 (1986):62–73. Traces Morrison's use of community in her protagonists' quests for wholeness. Believes Morrison's failure to bring Jadine and Son together at the end of *Tar Baby* suggests there is no place for folk tradition in modern black society.

Crouch, Stanley. "Aunt Medea." *New Republic,* 19 October 1987, 38–43. Diatribe against Morrison presented under the guise of a review of *Beloved,* which he describes as a "blackface holocaust novel."

Davis, Cynthia. "Self, Society and Myth in Toni Morrison's Fiction." *Contemporary Literature* 23 (1982):323–42. Surveys of tension between individual and societal commitment/demand in *The Bluest Eye, Sula,* and *Song of Solomon.*

Dowling, Colette. "Song of Toni Morrison." *New York Times Magazine,* 20 May 1979, 40–42. Brief plot summaries and biographical data.

de Weever, Jacqueline. "The Inverted World of Toni Morrison's *The Bluest Eye* and *Sula.*" *CLA Journal* 22 (1979):402–14. Discusses Morrisonian inversions in *The Bluest Eye* and *Sula.*

Edelberg, Cynthia Dubin. "Morrison's Voice: Formal Education, the Work Ethic, and the Bible." *American Literature* 58 (1986):217–37. Argues that the underlying message of four Morrison novels is that religion, formal education, and work amounts to nothing for black Americans; too excessive to be convincing.

Freiert, William K. "Classical Themes in Toni Morrison's *Song of Solomon.*" *Helios* 10 (1983):161–70. Finds allusions to five classical myths, including Ulysses, Oedipus, Mother-Earth, Daedalus, and Orpheus, in *Song of Solomon.*

Harper, Michael, and Robert Stepto, eds. "Interview." *Chant of Saints,* 213–29. Urbana: University of Illinois Press, 1979.

Harris A. Leslie. "Myth as Structure in Toni Morrison's *Song of Solomon.*" *Melus* 7 (1980):69–76. Discusses operations of mythic elements in *Song of Solomon.*

Hawthorne, Evelyn. "On Gaining the Double Vision: *Tar Baby* as Diasporean Novel." *Black American Literature Forum* 22 (1988):97–107. Discusses Son's diasporean awareness in *Tar Baby.*

Hovet, Grace Ann, and Barbara Lounsberry. "Flying as Symbol and Legend in Toni Morrison's *The Bluest Eye, Sula,* and *Song of Solomon.*" CLA Journal XXVII 2(1983):119–140. Discusses Morrison's adaptation of a traditional African mythology.

———. "Principles of Perception in Toni Morrison's *Sula. Black American Literature Forum* 13 (1979):126–29. Raises significant questions about preserving cultural identity in the world of flux that is found in Morrison's fiction.

Hudson-Weems, Clenora. "The World of Topsy-Turvydom in Toni Morrison's Fiction: A Methodological Explication of New Black Literary Criticism." *Western Journal of Black Studies* 10 (1986):132–36. Analysis of the level of existence of Morrison's characters whose personalities and actions are firmly grounded in an upside-down (topsy-turvy) perspective of Western culture.

Klotman, Phyllis R. "Dick-and-Jane and the Shirley Temple Sensibility in *The Bluest Eye.*" *Black American Literature Forum* 13 (1979)123–25. Study of the structure of *The Bluest Eye.*

Lange, Bonnie Shipman. "Toni Morrison's Rainbow Code." *Critique* 24 (1983):173–81. Detailed study of the colors and their symbolic significance in Morrison's work.

Lee, Dorothy H. "*Song of Solomon:* To Ride the Air." *Black American Literature Forum* 16 (1982):64–70. Argues that in *Song of Solomon* one finds a pilgrimage that has elements of the monomyth: initiation, renunciation, atonement, and relief.

Lee, Valerie Gray. "The Use of Folktalk in Novels by Black Women Writers." *CLA Journal* 23 (1980):266–72. A very sketchy study of the use of folktale in the novels of three women, including Morrison's *Sula.*

Lupton, Mary Jane. "Clothes and Closure in Three Novels by Black Women." *Black American Literature Forum* 20 (1986)409–21. Discusses the significance of clothing in Morrison's first three novels.

Marshall, Brenda. "The Gospel According to Pilate." *American Literature* 57(1985):486–89. Brief character study of Pilate, emphasizing her unique status as true pariah.

Martin, Odette. "*Sula.*" *First World* 1 (1977):34–44. Discussion of the life of Bottomites in *Sula.*

Mickelson, Anne Z. "Toni Morrison." *Reaching Out: Sensitivity and Order in Recent American Fiction by Women.* Metuchen, New Jersey: Scarecrow Press,

1979. Discusses the quest motif in *Sula* and *Song of Solomon* and also the classical theme of "earth mother."

Middleton, Victoria. "Sula: An Experimental Life." *College Language Association Journal* 28 (1985):367–81. A detailed analysis of the individuation of Sula.

Miller, Adam D. "Breedlove, Peace and the Dead: Some Observations on the World of Toni Morrison." *Black Scholar* 9 (1978):47–50.

Miner, Madonne. "Lady No Longer Sings the Blues: Rape, Madness and Silence in *The Bluest Eye*." *Conjuring: Black Women Fiction and Literary Tradition*, edited by Marjorie Pryse and Hortense J. Spillers. Bloomington, Indiana: Indiana University Press, 1985, 176–91. Study of female violation as literary theme, which she traces to ancient Greek mythology. She compares Pecola's experience with Philomela.

Nichols, Julie. "Patterns in Toni Morrison's Novels." *English Journal* 72(1983):46–48. Introductory level interpretation of Morrison's first three novels.

Ogunyemi, Chiwenye. "Order and Disorder in Toni Morrison's *The Bluest Eye*." *Critique, Studies in Modern Fiction* 19(1977):112–20. Examines the triadic patterns used by Morrison as structure in *The Bluest Eye*.

———. "*Sula*: 'A Nigger Joke.'" *Black American Literature Forum* 13(1979): 130–34. Study of ironies in lives and experiences of the blacks of Medallion.

Otten, Terry. "The Crime of Innocence in Toni Morrison's *Tar Baby*." *Studies in American Fiction* 14(1986):153–64. Focuses on Morrison's indictment of excessive materialism in the lives of the protagonists and their culture.

Portales, Marco. "Toni Morrison's *The Bluest Eye*: Shirley Temple and Cholly." *The Centennial Review* 30 (1986):496–506. Close examination of Morrison's analysis of a demented personality in *The Bluest Eye*.

Randolph, Laura B. "The Magic of Toni Morrison." *Ebony* (July 1988):100, 102, 104, 108. General discussion of author and work, with focus on *Beloved*.

Reyes, Angelita. "Ancient Properties in the New World: The Paradox of the "Other" in Toni Morrison's *Tar Baby*." *Black Scholar* 17 (1986):19–25. Discussion of what writer calls Morrison's use of the landscapes of New and Old World culture, history, and cosmological beliefs.

Rosenberg, Ruth. "Seeds in the Hard Ground: Black Girlhood in *The Bluest Eye*." *Black American Literature Forum* 21 (1987):435–45. Discusses the survival techniques of the Breedloves and the McTeers in a hostile society.

Royster, Philip M. "A Priest and a Witch against the Spiders and the Snakes: Scapegoating in Toni Morrison's *Sula*." *Umoja, Scholarly Journal of Black Studies* 2 (1978):149–68. Discusses Morrison's treatment of Sula and Shadrack as communal scapegoats.

———. "*The Bluest Eye*." *First World* 1 (1977):34–44. Looks at aesthetic values in black community and discusses their use by characters in *The Bluest Eye*.

————. "Milkman's Flying: The Scapegoat Transcended in Toni Morrison's *Song of Solomon*." *CLA Journal* 24 (1982):419–40. Discusses Morrison's use of Milkman as a scapegoat-victim in relation to himself, family, society, and culture.

Samuels, Wilfred D. "Liminality and the Search for Self in Toni Morrison's *Song of Solomon*." *Minority Voices* 5 (1981):59–68. Traces the quest for self-hood of the protagonist using both Western traditional myths and the anthropological perspective of Van Gennep.

Skerrett, Joseph. "Recitation to the Griot: Storytelling and Learning in Toni Morrison's *Song of Solomon*." *Black Women, Fiction and Literary Tradition*, edited by Marjorie Pryse and Hortense J. Spillers. Bloomington: University of Indiana Press, 1985, 192–202. Analysis of Morrison's use of the art of storytelling in her novel.

Smith, Barbara. "Beautiful, Needed, Mysterious." *Freedomways* 14(1974):69–72. "Discusses Morrison's use of "mascon images" in *Sula*.

Smith, Valerie. "Toni Morrison's Narratives of Community." In *Self Discovery and Authority in Afro-American Narrative*. Cambridge, Mass.: Harvard University Press, 1987, 122–153. Study of Morrison's development of community in her first three novels.

————. "The Quest for and Discovery of Identity in Toni Morrison's *Song of Solomon*." *Southern Review* 21(1985):721–32. Explores Milkman's insights gained from key characters in the novel.

Spallino, Chiara. "*Song of Solomon:* An Adventure in Structure." *Callaloo* 8(1985):510–24. Argues that the novel epitomizes Morrison's conviction that blacks have to cling to their cultural identity to fight the American system.

Spillers, Hortense J. "A Hateful Passion, A Love Lost." In *Feminist Issues in Literary Scholarship*, edited by Shari Bernstock. Bloomington: Indiana University Press, 1987. Compares *Sula* with two novels by black women novelists. Spillers is interested in the psychological progression of black women as revealed in these texts.

Stein, Karen F. " 'I Didn't Even Know His Name': Names and Naming in Toni Morrison's *Sula*." *Names* (1980):226–29. Offers close reading of the symbolic significance of names in *Sula*.

————. "Toni Morrison's *Sula:* A Black Woman's Epic." *Black American Literature Forum* (1984):146–50. Sees *Sula* as an innovative black woman's epic.

Strouse, Jean. "Toni Morrison's Black Magic." *Newsweek,* 30 March 1981, 52–57. General commentary on author's work and useful biographical information.

Turner, Darwin T. "Theme, Characterization, and Style in the Works of Toni

Morrison." *Black Women Writers (1950–1980), A Critical Evaluation,* edited by Mari Evans. New York: Doubleday, 1984, 361–70. Examines Morrison's masterful use of these traditional elements of fiction and how they make her a major novelist.

Wegs, Joyce M. "Toni Morrison's *Song of Solomon:* A Blues Song." *Essays in Literature* 9 (1982):211–23. Study of the functionality of fiction, which, like the blues, is a vehicle for articulating and handing down historical concepts and cultural values.

Weixlman, Joe. "Cultural Clash, Survival, and Transformation: A Study of Some Innovative Afro-American Novels of Detection." *Mississippi Quarterly* 38 (1984–85):21–32. Identifies the influence of the modern South American novel—the tradition of "magical reality"—and demonstrates its effectiveness in Morrison's story.

Willis, Susan. "Eruption of Funk: Historicizing Toni Morrison." *Black American Literature Forum* 16 (1982):34–41. Argues that Morrison uses varied forms of disruption and intrusion in her novels.

Index